ONE CLASSROOM, MANY CULTURES

Cross-Curricular Lesson Plans for Embracing Cultural Diversity

Authors: Jonathan Gross
Deborah Kopka
Bonnie J. Krueger
Cover and Book Design: Patti Jeffers

© 2009 Lorenz Educational Press,
a Lorenz company, and its licensors.
All rights reserved

Permission to photocopy the student activities in this book is hereby granted to one teacher as part of the purchase price. This permission may only be used to provide copies for this teacher's specific classroom setting. This permission may not be transferred, sold, or given to any additional or subsequent user of this product. Thank you for respecting copyright laws.

Printed in the United States of America

978-1-4291-0408-1

BRIDGING
the Gaps in Education™
Lorenz Educational Press

How to Use This Book

Embark on an international journey… within the walls of your classroom! *One Classroom, Many Cultures* is a set of informational articles and cross-curricular activities to enhance your students' knowledge and interest in other parts of the world. Learn about each country's history, customs, special holidays, cuisine, leisure activities, and entertainment, and then reinforce the students' understanding with the games and reproducible worksheets provided. Additional extension activities are also included at the end of the resource. *Bienvenidos! Irashaimasu! Fáilte! Swaagatam! Welcome!*

National Standards

The articles and activities in this book address the following National Education Standards:

Social Sciences

NSS-WH.5-12.2 Early Civilizations and the Emergence of Pastoral People, 4000-1000 BCE

NSS-WH.5-12.3 Classical Traditions, Major Religions, and Giant Empires, 1000 B.C.E.E-300 BCE

NSS-WH.5-12.4 Expanding Zones of Exchange and Encounter, 300-100 CE

NSS-WH.5-12.5 Intensified Hemispheric Interactions, 1000-1500 CE

NSS-WH.5-12.6 The Emergence of the First Global Age, 1450-1770

NSS-WH.5-12.7 An Age of Revolutions, 1750-1914

NSS-WH.5-12.9 The 20th Century Since 1945: Promises and Paradoxes

NSS-G.K-12.1 The World in Spatial Terms

NSS-G.K-12.4 Human Systems

NSS-G.K-12.5 Environment and Society

NSS-G.K-12.6 The Uses of Geography

NSS-USH.K-4.4 The History of Peoples of Many Cultures Around the World

NSS-USH.5-12.1 Three Worlds Meet (Beginnings to 1620)

Science

NS.5-8.6 Personal and Social Perspectives

Language Arts

NL-ENG.K-12.1 Reading for Perspective

NL-ENG.K-12.5 Communication Strategies

NL-ENG.K-12.8 Developing Research Skills

NL-ENG.K-12.9 Multicultural Understanding

Table of Contents

Mexico
FAST FACTS: Mexico 4
A History of Mexico 6
Everyday Mexico 8
Mexican Celebrations! (Fiestas!) 10
Mathematics… Mayan-Style! 11
Mapping Out History - Mexico 12
La Lotería 13

India
FAST FACTS: India 15
A History of India 17
Everyday India 19
Indian Celebrations! 21
Gandhi Timeline 22
Indian Food Favorites 23
Try Your Hand at Hindi 24

Japan
FAST FACTS: Japan 25
A History of Japan 26
Everyday Japan 27
Japanese Celebrations! (Matsuri!) 29
Mapping Out History - Japan 30
Haiku 31
Origami 32

Egypt
FAST FACTS: Egypt 33
A History of Egypt 35
Everyday Egypt 37
Egyptian Celebrations! 39
The Pyramids 40
A Difference of Customs 41
Translating English to Hieroglyphics 42

Ireland
FAST FACTS: Ireland 43
A History of Ireland 44
Everyday Ireland 46
Irish Celebrations! (Hooleys!) 48
Mapping Out History - Ireland 49
Limerick 50
Next Stop: Ireland! 51

Australia
FAST FACTS: Australia 52
A History of Australia 54
Everyday Australia 56
Australian Celebrations! 58
Create Your Own Flag 59
Australian Phrases 60
Creating Symbols 61

Extension Ideas and Additional Resources 62

Answer Keys 64

FAST FACTS: Mexico

Full Name: United Mexican States (Estados Unidos Mexicanos)
Capital City: Mexico City
Currency: Mexican peso

Location

Mexico is located at the southern part of North America. Covering nearly 760,000 square miles, Mexico shares a northern border with the United States and a southeastern border with Guatemala and Belize in South America. To the west of Mexico lies the Pacific Ocean, and the Gulf of Mexico and the Caribbean Sea run along much of the country's eastern coastline.

The People

Throughout history, many groups of Native Americans have lived on the land we now call Mexico. Descendents of many of these groups, including the Aztecs, Mayans, and Toltecs, continue to live in Mexico today. But *mestizos*, or people of European and Native American ancestry, make up the largest part of the Mexican population. Today, more than 100 million people of all backgrounds live in Mexico.

Spanish is the official language of Mexico, but nearly 100 native languages are also spoken. Mayan and Nahuatl (noo-WAHT-uhl) are both languages commonly heard in different parts of the country.

The Government
Mexico's government is very similar to the United States government in many ways. It is divided into 3 branches: the executive branch, consisting of the president and his/her cabinet; the legislative branch, made up of the Senate and the Chamber of Deputies; and the judicial branch, which has a Supreme Court at its highest level. The country is divided into 31 states and a federal district that contains the capital—Mexico City.

The Land
Nearly 2/3 of Mexico is covered with hills and mountains. The Sierra Madre is the largest mountain range in the country, and it is divided into 3 smaller ranges. A group of more than 20 volcanoes called the Trans-Mexican Volcanic Belt links sections of the ranges of the Sierra Madre. Mexico is home to more than 40 volcanoes, many of which remain active.

Mexico is also home to hot deserts, sandy beaches, vast canyons, and ancient ruins. Popular tourist attractions include the beaches of Acapulco and Cancun, the ruins of Chichén Itzá (chee-CHEN eet-SAH), and the historic city of Guadalajara.

The Flag
The Mexican flag is filled with symbolism:

Green stripe—hope and victory

White stripe—purity

Red stripe—blood shed by heroes

Eagle emblem—According to legend, an Aztec god described the location of the new empire as the place where an eagle stands on a prickly pear tree with a serpent in its mouth. The Aztecs found the eagle on a small island in the middle of a lake. This is where the Aztec capital Tenochtitlan (tay-NOWSH-teet-LAHN), now Mexico City, was built.

A History of Mexico

Mexico's history is a long and often tragic one. From the Mixtecs to the Aztecs, the Spanish conquerors to the Mexican rebels, Mexico has remained strong in times of great conflict.

Mesoamerica, an area that is now southern Mexico and Central America, was home to many different groups of people. While some of these groups were very small, others were larger and made major changes to the history of the country. Today, many people living in Mexico are descendents of these groups. Below is a short introduction to the major groups of Native Americans and their place in the history of Mexico.

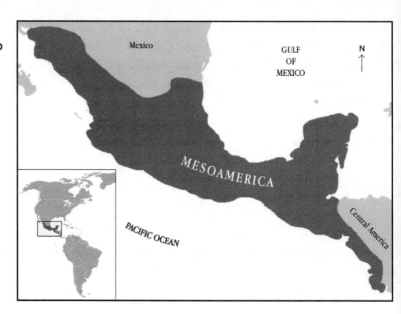

The Olmecs, Zapotecs, and Mixtecs

These three cultures are some of the earliest to occupy Mesoamerica. Focused mainly on farming and fishing, the Olmec society was known for its giant stone sculptures of human heads. Although the exact years of the Olmec's presence are unknown, it is thought that they lived around 1300 B.C.E. to 400 B.C.E..

The Zapotec people were in Mesoamerica from around 200 B.C.E. to 800 C.E. They designed the first system of writing in North America and were skilled pottery-makers. The Zapotecs also had their own language.

Using pictures drawn on deerskin or bark paper, the Mixtecs recorded a very detailed history of their life in Mesoamerica. From 700-1500 C.E., they produced some of the finest products of stone and metal in ancient Mexico. The Mixtecs were engaged in constant warfare with other tribes in the area, including the Zapotecs, and later, the Aztecs.

The Mayans and the Toltecs

Considered to be the most advanced empire of Mesoamerica, the Mayan people were known for their work in math, astronomy, and architecture. This powerful nation created large cities and built pyramids that stood over 200 feet tall. The Mayans were also responsible for creating a complex calendar system to mark important dates. From around 300-900 C.E., the Mayan culture lived in what is now southern Mexico and Central America.

The Toltec people were excellent builders and metalworkers during their history in Mexico (900-1200 C.E.). They are thought to have been related to the Zapotec and Mixtec people. Even though the Toltecs took over parts of the Mayan empire, their reign only lasted a few hundred years.

The Aztecs

The Aztecs, also called the Mexica, were a group known to be fierce warriors. Even though they started as a small group of native people, more than 5 million Aztecs were soon in Mesoamerica. This large civilization combined with the people of nearby cities to form the "Triple Alliance", which was large enough to conquer much of central and southern Mexico. The Aztecs soon became the most powerful group in the country.

Spanish Conquest

A group of Spanish explorers led by Hernán Cortés arrived in 1519. They claimed the land in the name of Spain and conquered the native people. Cities were invaded, treasure was stolen, and many items were destroyed by the Spanish. The country was renamed "New Spain", and the native people were forced into slavery. The Spanish brought diseases with them to New Spain that killed nearly 24 million people.

Rebellion

In 1810, a native priest named Miguel Hidalgo y Costilla (coh-STEE-yah) called for a revolution. He, along with many other natives of New Spain, wanted freedom from the wealthy Spaniards that controlled much of their country. These natives, or *criollos* (cree-OH-yohs), formed an army and went to war with Spain. On September 21, 1821, after 11 years of battle, New Spain was given its independence and renamed *Mexico*.

A New Nation

Over the next several decades, the new country of Mexico had many problems. Several wars were fought to maintain the independence of the nation, including the Texas War in 1836 and the Pastry War in 1838. The Mexican-American War in 1846 resulted in the Treaty of Guadalupe Hidalgo, which gave the land that is now Texas, Colorado, California, Arizona, Nevada, New Mexico, and parts of Wyoming and Utah to the United States.

In the late 1800s, Porfirio Diaz, the president of Mexico, was unfairly supporting the wealthy landowners while many Mexican citizens grew very poor. In 1910, a ten-year Civil War began as a reaction to Diaz's rule. Over 2 million people died during this war. In the end, a new president was elected, but the fight for peace was not yet won.

Mexico joined forces with the United States during World War II. Their work gained them money to use for education and helped many poor families. But Mexico still had many problems, and fighting continued within the country. In 2000, Vincente Fox Quesada was elected president of Mexico. He formed a new type of government to help build better lives for the people of Mexico. Even though the country continues to have difficult times, it is moving toward a more peaceful future.

Everyday Mexico

Food

Mexican food is a combination of native Mexican and Spanish dishes introduced to the country in the 1500s. Each area of the country has its own special cooking style and favorite recipes.

The most important item in Mexican food is corn. Eaten at nearly every meal, corn is used to make tortillas, which are like thin pancakes. Corn is also used in many common Mexican dishes:

Enchiladas—rolled tortillas stuffed with meat, cheese, and covered with chili sauce

Tamales—meat and vegetables wrapped in corn husks

Burritos—enchiladas without chili sauce

Tortas—Mexican sandwiches

Quesadillas—fried tortillas folded in half and filled with cheese

Other common ingredients in Mexican food include beans, rice, squash, tomatoes, avocados, potatoes, and plantains. Chili peppers are also a very important ingredient in Mexican food—they provide spicy heat to any meal!

Clothing

Mexican clothing is usually divided into modern, traditional, and celebration costumes. In larger towns and cities, most people wear clothes similar to those seen in the U.S., such as t-shirts, jeans, and sneakers. More traditional Mexican clothing includes wide-brimmed hats called *sombreros* (sohm-BRAYR-ohs) and shawls called *serapes* (sehr-OHP-ays). Traditional clothing is usually hand woven and often brightly colored.

Costumes worn during *fiestas* (celebrations) can be very elaborate. Women wear long, colorful skirts that twirl around them as they dance. Men often wear *charro*, or rodeo costumes, which include embroidered pants, a shirt, a jacket, and often a hat.

Art and Literature

Mexican art dates back thousands of years, from the giant sculptures created by the Olmecs to the jewelry and pottery of the Aztecs. Museums in Mexico are home to many pieces of art created by these ancient cultures, and it is here that the history of Mexican art can still be seen today.

Modern Mexican artists are often known for their murals, or wall paintings. Diego Rivera, David Siqueiros, and Jose Orozco were painters that often showed the struggles of the Mexican people in their murals. Frida Kahlo, Diego Rivera's wife, was also a famous Mexican painter.

Many people in Mexico make their living by creating art. Certain areas in Mexico are known for their silver jewelry. People in other places create pottery, clothing, wooden carvings, and glassware.

Several of the world's most famous authors have come from Mexico. In 1990, Octavio Paz won a Nobel Prize in Literature for his poetry about Mexican life. Other Mexican writers have sold millions of books around the world, many of which tell stories of Mexican history and culture.

Sports

Fútbol (FOOT-bohl)—Soccer
This is the most popular sport in Mexico. Not only does Mexico have schools across the country with their own teams that compete against each other, but the country also has a professional soccer league. The soccer championship, called the World Cup, takes place every four years and is often hosted by Mexico.

Béisbol (BEHS-bohl)—Baseball
Second only to *fútbol*, baseball is a very popular sport in Mexico. This sport was introduced to the country by the United States in the early 1900s. Since then many Mexican baseball players have joined professional U.S. teams.

Bullfighting
Mexico boasts more than 200 bullrings that serve as home to the ancient sport of bullfighting. Introduced by Spanish conquerors in the 16th century, bullfighting continues to be an intense (and very popular) spectator sport in Mexico, as well as in Spain and other parts of Latin America. *Matadors* wave a bright red cape as angry bulls charge back and forth during the event.

Charreada (char-ay-AH-dah)
This is a very old Mexican tradition that is similar to a rodeo. Tricks on horseback and roping stunts are performed by *charros* (CHAR-rohs) dressed in fancy costumes. The charreada begins with a parade and ends with a great celebration.

Music, Dance, and Games

Mariachi (mahr-ee-AH-chee) is a traditional Mexican music band made up of 6 to 8 members. They stroll around plazas and restaurants and play music for a small fee. The instruments in a mariachi band can vary, but the guitar, horn, and violin are all common.

Norteño music is usually played by an accordion and guitar. This style is like country-western music, and different regions of Mexico have their own version of norteño. A similar type of music, called *tejano*, is a combination of norteño, polka, blues, and pop music.

Dancing is very popular in Mexico, and it takes place at nearly all celebrations. *Matachin* dancers carry brightly colored swords while shaking a gourd rattle. These dancers often wear tall headdresses and colored ribbons. *Conchero* dancers wear elaborate costumes and perform traditional dances at fiestas around the country. There are also troupes of ballet *dancers* throughout Mexico.

El Jarabe Tapatío, often called the Mexican Hat Dance, is thought to be the national dance of Mexico. During the dance, men in rodeo costumes dance around a sombrero (wide-brimmed hat) while women twirl in colorful dresses.

Mexican Celebrations! (Fiestas!)

Day of Saint Anthony the Abbot
January 17th

In honor of Saint Anthony, this holiday is a celebration for children—and their pets! Every year, children bathe, brush, and dress up their pets in preparation for this day. The pets are paraded around town before they are taken to a church to be blessed by a priest. Dogs, cats, goldfish, chickens, and even burros (donkeys) take part in this event!

Cinco de Mayo (sin-COH dey MY-oh)–Fifth of May
May 5th

In 1862, French troops were sent to conquer Mexico by Napoleon III. This large military force was defeated by a small Mexican army at the Battle of Puebla. The victory is honored every year with a nationwide celebration, including parades, food, and dancing. Cinco de Mayo is often confused with Mexico's Independence Day, which is actually celebrated on September 16th.

Independence Day
September 16th

Mexico declared its independence from Spain on this day in 1821. Shouts of *"Viva México!"* (*"Long live Mexico!"*) fill the air as parades, rodeos, and fireworks mark the occasion.

Día de los Muertos (DEE-ah dey lohs MWEHR-tohs)–Day of the Dead
November 2nd

Dia de los Muertos is a day for families to honor their deceased relatives. Many believe that the spirits of these relatives return to Earth during this joyful celebration. Children enjoy candies in the shape of human skulls, and bakers make *Pan de los Muertos*, or Bread of the Dead. Flowers and other small trinkets are brought to the graves as gifts, while families celebrate with a picnic nearby. At night, candles are often lit to help guide the spirits to their resting place.

Día de Nuestra Senora de Guadalupe (DEE-ah dey noo-ES-trah sen-YOHR-ah dey gwad-ah-LOO-pay)–Guadalupe Day
December 12th

This is one of the most important religious holidays in Mexico. It is said that in the year 1531, the patron saint of Mexico appeared to a peasant in a vision. She told the peasant, Juan Diego, to have a church built in her honor. Every year, millions of pilgrims travel to Mexico City to see the church, the Basilica of the Virgin of Guadalupe, and to pray together.

Christmas
December 25th

Christmas in Mexico is actually celebrated for much of December and January. From December 16th to December 25th, a series of nightly candlelight processions take place to reenact the journey of Mary and Joseph to Bethlehem. These processions end at a chosen house in the neighborhood, where a party (called a *posada*) then begins. A big part of the posada (poh-SAH-dah) is the *piñata* (pin-YAH-tah). This star-shaped container is filled with toys and candy and struck by blindfolded children with a stick until it breaks open. Piñatas can also be found during birthday parties and other celebrations.

Three Kings Day
January 6th

Also a part of Christmas, *Three Kings Day* celebrates the day it is thought that the Wise Men arrived at the manger in Bethlehem. Children in Mexico are usually given gifts on this day to represent the gifts given to baby Jesus by the Wise Men. In some parts of the country, children leave their shoes by the door in hopes that the generous Wise Men will leave gifts for them. *Rosca de los Reyes* (king's ring) is a special cake often baked in celebration of this holiday.

Name _____   Date _____

Mathematics... Mayan-Style!

The Mayan system of writing numbers used dots, bars, and a symbol that looks like a shell. A Mayan numbering chart is listed below. Use this chart to solve the various math problems. Be sure to write your answers in Mayan numerals!

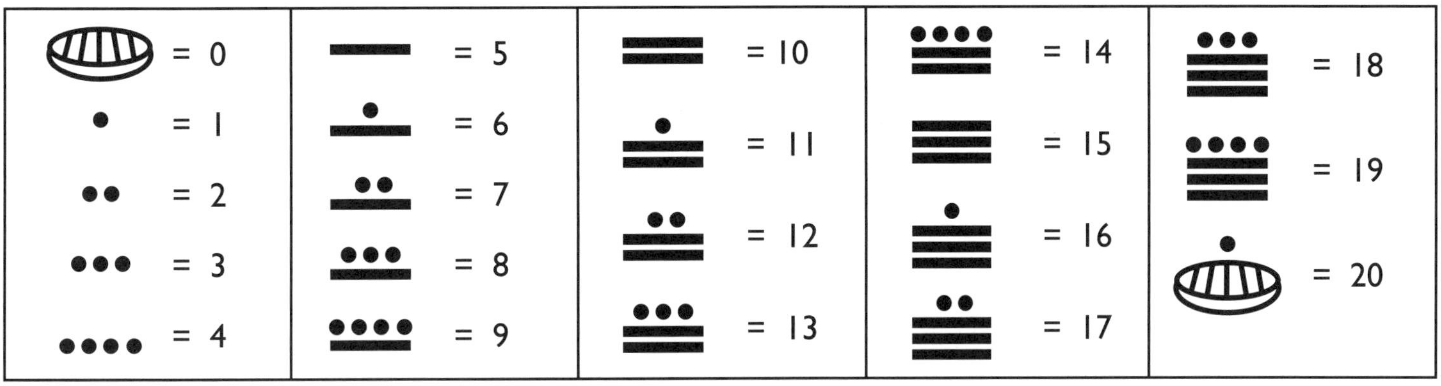

shell = 0	— = 5	≡ = 10	••••/≡ = 14	•••/≡≡ = 18
• = 1	•/— = 6	•/≡ = 11	—/≡ = 15	••••/≡≡ = 19
•• = 2	••/— = 7	••/≡ = 12	•/—/≡ = 16	•/shell = 20
••• = 3	•••/— = 8	•••/≡ = 13	••/—/≡ = 17	
•••• = 4	••••/— = 9	••••/≡ = 13		

Addition

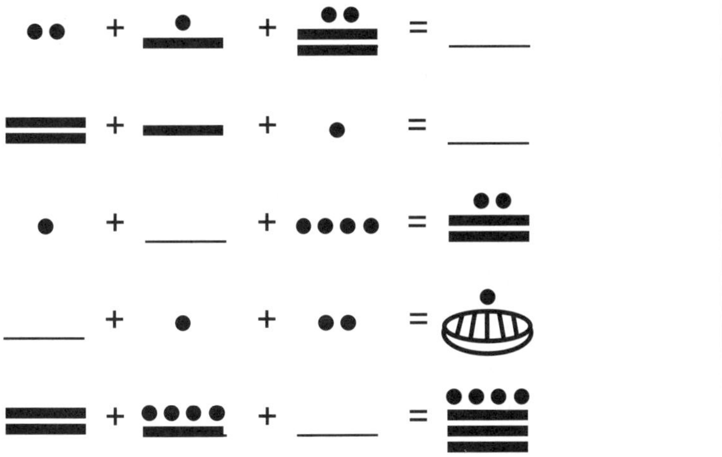

•• + •/— + ••/— = ____

≡ + — + • = ____

• + ____ + •••• = ••/≡

____ + • + •• = shell

≡ + ••••/— + ____ = ••••/≡

Multiplication

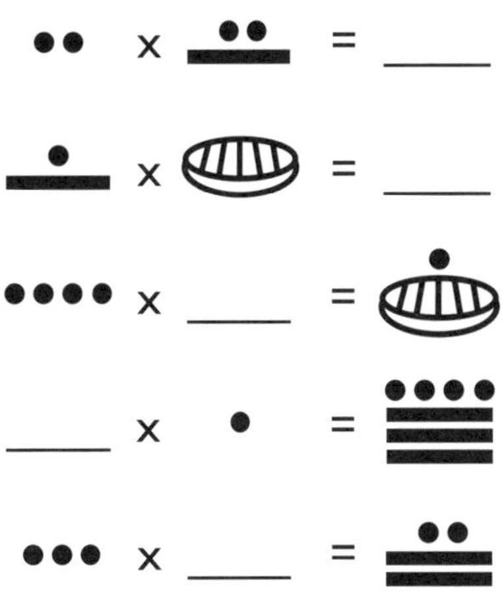

•• × ••/— = ____

•/— × shell = ____

•••• × ____ = shell

____ × • = ••••/≡

••• × ____ = ••/≡

Subtraction

•/shell − •••/— = ____

••••/— − — − •••• = ____

____ − •• − ••• = ____

••••/— − ••• − ____ = ••••

••••/≡ − ____ = •• •• ••

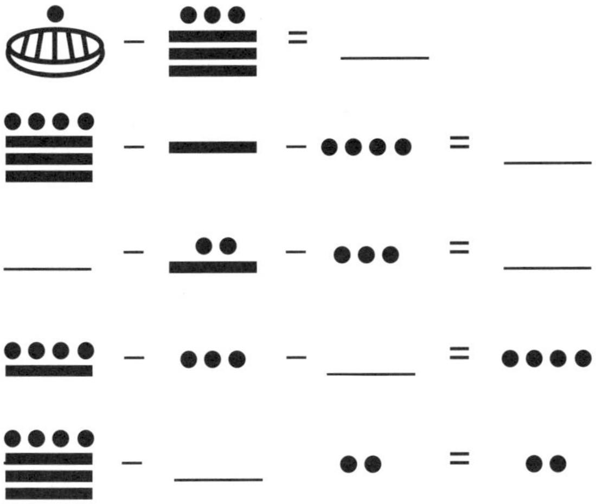

Division

•••/— ÷ •• = ____

•/≡ ÷ •••• = ____

shell ÷ ____ = ≡

____ ÷ — = ••••

≡ ÷ ____ = •••

11

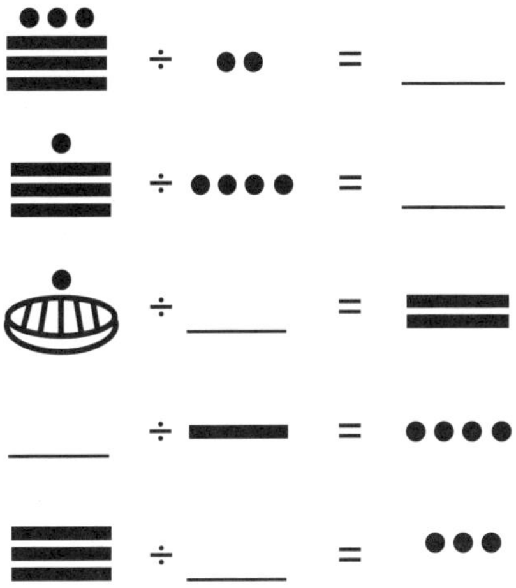

Mapping Out History - Mexico

Use the map of Mexico to record some of the country's most influential people and places in history. Begin by labeling a few of Mexico's natural features, and then add the historic locations.

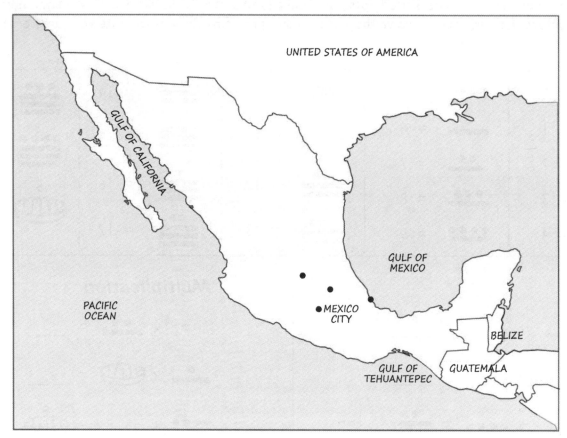

1. From about 1300-400 B.C.E., the Olmecs lived on the land north of the Gulf of Tehuantepec (tay-WAHN-teh-pehk). Shade this area red.

2. Around 300-900 AD, the Maya lived in much of what is now Guatemala and Belize. They also lived in the Yucatan Peninsula, which is the land north of Guatemala and Belize. Label the Yucatan Peninsula, and shade the land of the Mayans blue.

3. The Aztec capital of Tenochtitlan (tay-NOWSH-teet-LAHN) was located (from 1325-1521) in the same place that Mexico City now stands. Label Tenochtitlan on the map.

4. Teotihuacán (tay-oh-tee-wah-KAHN) was one of the largest cities of ancient Mexico. It was located northeast of Tenochtitlan. Label Teotihuacán on the map.

5. The Aztecs and Toltecs both lived in the area surrounding Teotihuacán at different points in history. Shade this area on the map green.

6. Hernán Cortés landed at Veracruz, a city east of Tenochtitlan, in 1519. Label Veracruz on the map.

7. Miguel Hidalgo y Costillas called for a rebellion in 1810 from the small village of Dolores, northwest of Teotihuacán. Label Dolores on the map.

8. The Sierra Madre mountain ranges are found along Mexico's west coast from the Gulf of California to the Gulf of Tehuantepec, and on the east coast from the US-Mexico border to Veracruz. Label the mountain ranges with Xs.

9. The Trans-Mexican Volcanic Belt runs west to east across central Mexico, slightly north of Mexico City. Label this belt using ∆s.

La Lotería

(lah loh-tehr-EE-ah)

This game of chance was brought to Mexico from Spain in the late 18th century and is still commonly played at festivals throughout the country. Similar to Bingo, La Lotería is played on a 9- or 16-square grid containing a random assortment of pictures. These pictures are also found on cards put into a bag and drawn by the *caller*. The traditional La Lotería game is played with a specific set of 54 pictures, all of which have riddles associated with them. The game below is a variation on the traditional game that can be played with your students.

Materials (per student):
1 copy of *La Loteria* on page 14
9 game markers (paper clips, pennies, small candies, etc.)

Directions:

Read through all of the pictures of common Mexican ingredients on the Lotería cards with the students. Have the students select any 9 of the pictures to draw (or write the word for) within the grid. After the students have completed their grids, randomly select an ingredient from the list and read it aloud. Everyone that has that picture on his or her grid should cover it with a game marker. Continue calling the ingredients. When a student has completely covered their grid, have them shout "¡Lotería!"

Ingredients to call:

- Queso (KAY-soh)—cheese
- Frijoles (free-HOH-lehs)—beans
- Maiz (my-EES)—corn
- Leche (LAY-cheh)—milk
- Tomate (toh-MAH-tay)—tomato
- Plátano (PLAH-tah-noh)—plantain
- Papa (PAH-pah)—potato
- Aguacate (ah-gwah-KAH-tay)—avocado
- Pan (pahn)—bread
- Helado (ay-LAH-doh)—ice cream
- Pescado (pays-KAH-doh)—fish
- Café (kah-FAY)—coffee
- Arroz (ayr-ROHS)—rice
- Calabacita (cah-lah-bah-SEE-tah)—squash
- Pollo (POH-yoh)—chicken
- Chocolate (choh-koh-LAH-tay)—chocolate

In Your Own Words

Select one of the following writing prompts and have the students write a paragraph or small essay in response:

- *El Jarabe Tapatío* is a very popular folk dance, and is often considered the national dance of Mexico. What dance would you choose to be the national dance of your home country? Why? Describe the dance and any costumes or props needed to perform it. If you would like, you can even make up a new dance!

- Octavio Paz won a Nobel Prize for his poetry about Mexico. Write a short poem describing some of the best things about your country or specific state. (Teachers: You may want to select a certain poetry form for the students to write, such as acrostic or haiku).

- Soccer, or *fútbol*, is the most popular sport in Mexico. What is your favorite sport? Would you rather play or watch this sport? Is your favorite sport played in other countries too? (Teachers: You may wish to have the students research their sport to find additional information.)

LA LOTERÍA

Pollo Chicken

Plátano Plantain

Café Coffee

Maiz Corn

Queso Cheese

Aguacate Avocado

Calabacita Squash

Tomate Tomato

Pescado Fish

Pan Bread

Chocolate Chocolate

Papa Potato

Arroz Rice

Leche Milk

Frijoles Beans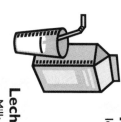

Helado Ice Cream

FAST FACTS: India

Full Name: *Republic of India*
Capital City: *New Delhi*
Currency: *Indian rupee*

Location

India, which is in Southern Asia, is the seventh largest country in the world. Most of India forms a peninsula with water on three sides. The Indian Ocean lies to the south, the Arabian Sea to the west, and the Bay of Bengal to the east. Pakistan is its western land neighbor. China, Nepal, and Bhutan are its northeastern neighbors. Myanmar (formerly called Burma) and Bangladesh are to the east. India is about one-third of the size of the United States.

The People

India has many races and cultures with a population close to 1,148,000,000 people. We don't know the exact origin of Indian people, but humans are believed to have lived in the northwestern Himalayas about 14 million years ago.

In India, there are six main ethnic groups. *Negritos*, the earliest people to come to India, were from Africa. Some of their descendants now live in the southern part of mainland India. The *Austrics* came next and are considered the founders of Indian civilization. Their languages are still spoken in central and eastern India. The *Mongoloids* in northeastern India generally resemble Asian people in their facial structure and skin color. *Dravidians* are the people of southern India. *Western Bracycephals* live mainly on the western side of the country. And *Nordics*, the last group to immigrate to India between 2000 and 1500 B.C.E., are now in northern and central India.

As a result of its many ethnic groups, India has 22 officially recognized languages. About 30 percent of the people speak Hindi, which is the official language of the government. English is an associate official language. Sanskrit, the ancient language of India that is 5,000 years old, is the basis of many modern Indian languages, including Hindi. All classical literature in India was written in Sanskrit.

15

The Government

India is a republic with 28 states. It has three branches of government: the legislative branch, the executive branch, and the judicial branch.

The head of state is the President of India. An electoral college that consists of elected members of both houses of Parliament and the legislatures of the states elects the President for a five-year term. After the elections, the Parliamentary members of the majority party choose the Prime Minister, who has more executive power than the President.

India's legislature is a Parliament that consists of the upper house, called the Council of States, and the lower house, called the House of People. The Council of States has 245 members who are elected for six-year terms by the Indian states. 543 of the House of People's 545 members are elected for five-year terms to represent their individual districts; the other two are nominated by the President.

The President, Vice President, and the Council of Ministers compose the executive branch. The Prime Minister heads the Council of Ministers.

India's judiciary branch consists of a Supreme Court, 21 High Courts, and many trial courts. Like the U.S. Supreme Court, the Supreme Court of India is the ultimate court that interprets the Constitution.

The Land

India is a land of extreme contrasts. In the north and northeast are the Himalayan Mountains, the world's tallest mountain range. The Indo-Gangetic Plain (a large, fertile area) occupies most of northern and eastern India. The region is named after the Indus and the Ganges, the two main rivers there. The Deccan Plateau occupies most of southern India. In the west is the Thar Desert, also called the Great Indian Desert.

Because the land is so diverse—ranging from mountains to deserts, rainforests, and plateaus—the climate ranges from very cold to very hot and tropical. The four seasons include winter (January and February), summer (March to May), a monsoon (rainy) season from June to September, and a post-monsoon season from October to December. Droughts are common, as are floods from the monsoons.

The Flag

The National Flag of India was adopted in 1947 and stands for freedom. It has three bars of color: saffron (orange) on the top for courage and sacrifice, white in the middle for purity and truth, and dark green at the bottom for faith and fertility. In the center of the flag, on the white band, is a spinning Chakra (*chakra* (SHAH-Krah) means *wheel* in Sanskrit). This ancient Buddhist symbol is meant to represent peaceful, positive change.

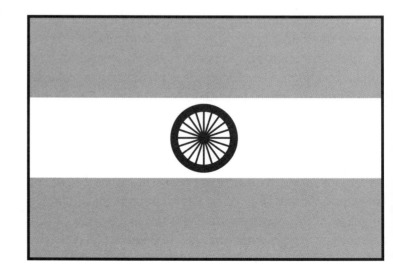

A History of India

Indus Valley Civilization

India's history began with the Indus Valley civilization in 2500 B.C.E., in what is today Pakistan and western India. Nothing was known about this culture until the 1920s, when India's Archaeological Department unearthed the ruins of two cities, Mohenjo daro (moh-HEN-joh DAHR-oh) and Harappa (hah-RAH-pay), in the Indus Valley. The buildings, household items, weapons, precious metals, toys, and other items indicate a highly civilized people who lived in this region 400,000 to 500,000 years ago. The Indus Valley civilization ended by 1500 B.C.E., due to the invasion of the Aryans, along with natural causes like floods and earthquakes.

Aryan and Greek Invasions

The Aryans, a group of nomadic tribes from central Asia, reached India around 200 B.C.E. and settled in modern-day northwest India. These first invaders spoke Sanskrit. Eventually, their way of life mingled with that of the local people. The culture that evolved became known as Hinduism—the spiritual philosophy that evolved from sacred texts called the Vedas. Hinduism remains one of the great religions of the world and one of the key religions in India.

Another great invasion occurred when the Persian Kings Cyrus and Darius conquered the Indus Valley. In 326 B.C.E., Alexander the Great, the Greek King and military commander, crossed the Indus but did not stay in India.

Ancient Dynasties

The history of ancient India is the history of the rise and fall of several dynasties, which are the reigns of the descendants of a particular family. Two dynasties figure heavily into ancient Indian history:

The Maurya (MOH-ree-yah) *Dynasty*, India's first, was founded by Chandragupta (chan-drah-GOOP-tah) Maurya. It reached its peak around 260 B.C.E. under Emperor Ashoka, India's most famous historical figure. During this time, India made contact with the outside world.

The Gupta Dynasty, which lasted from 320 C.E. to 480 C.E., is often called the Golden Age of Indian history. During this period in northern India, science, art, and culture grew. But by 455 C.E. the Huns had invaded India from the north and destroyed the Guptan Empire.

Middle Eastern and European Invasions

The Muslim influence in India today began during the Middle Ages when Muslims began to invade India from the Middle East toward the end of the 12th century. As in the ancient period, many dynasties ruled the country over the centuries. Established in the early 1500s, the Great Mughal (Mogul) Dynasty lasted until the 1700s. During this period, beautiful palaces, gardens, and tombs were created, including the magnificent Taj Mahal. Called one of the Wonders of the World, the Taj Mahal was built by an emperor as a tomb for his second wife and a symbol of their love.

India's rich natural resources, like diamonds and coal, made it a target for invasion by European countries. The Portuguese settled in the country in 1498. The Dutch, the British, and the French followed in the 1600s. The French and English fought over establishment of trade. After a final battle in 1757, the English established political control over India and held it until the 20th century.

Independence!

By the late 19th century, Indians longed to rule themselves. The most famous leader in this movement for independence was Mahatma Gandhi. He worked with other Indian leaders to end British colonial rule with nonviolent protests. Britain finally decided to leave India, and the country became completely independent in 1947.

Some Indian Muslims thought that an independent India would be led by Hindus. Following independence, India was divided to create the Muslim state of Pakistan. Terrible violence broke out. More than 1 million people were killed as 6 million Muslims moved toward Pakistan and 5 million Hindus moved toward India. Mahatma Gandhi opposed dividing the country. In 1948, he was assassinated by a Hindu who hated his support of Muslims.

In 1950, India became a republic with a new constitution. It is still coping with problems of overpopulation, poverty, and conflict with Pakistan. But the economy continues to improve and even thrive. India is known for exporting computer software and for many other technological industries. Its film industry—Bollywood—is the largest in the world!

Everyday India

Food

One thing is certain: you'll never forget the taste of Indian food! The dishes - ranging from mild to spicy, sweet to tart - are anything but bland. Indians use herbs and spices in all dishes from breakfast to dessert. Even Indian drinks are likely to contain sweet coconut juice, rich chocolate, rose petals, or nutmeg.

Chicken, fish, eggs, and lamb are some common dishes. But it is vegetarian food for which India is famous, since many of the country's religions prohibit eating meat. India has perfected the art of the meatless dish. It's famous for spicy curry, a dish made of savory cooked vegetables over rice. You're as likely to find curries in an Indian take-away (take-out) shop as you are to find them in someone's home.

Rice is a staple of all Indian diets. So is bread, which can be boiled, steamed, fried, or cooked on a griddle. A popular flat bread called *naan* (nahn) is cooked in a tandoor (clay) oven and eaten folded over. Sometimes ingredients like onions are baked into it.

Indian snacks include *samosas*, stuffed, deep-fried pockets of dough served with a spicy sauce called chutney. Desserts include *gulab jamun* (GOO-lohb YAY-moon), fried dough balls with a hot syrup drizzled over them. Favorite drinks include tea, coffee, milk with nuts and cardamom, and lemonade.

Sports

Wrestling, polo, archery, field hockey, and badminton are thought to have originated in India. Chess and card playing began there, too.

India loves sports! India has won eight Olympic gold medals in field hockey, which is the official national sport. Indians play soccer all year round. And tennis—both table tennis (ping-pong) and lawn tennis played on a court—has been popular since the British introduced the sports to the country in the 19th century.

But it is cricket (the British version of baseball) that is India's national obsession. The British brought cricket to India in the 18th century. Now nearly every Indian boy plays cricket. Indian cricket stars are treated like rock stars, and some of them become extremely wealthy. When India wins a cricket tournament, people shoot off fireworks in their yards!

Art & Literature

Much of the Indian art produced over the centuries was created to honor religious figures. A great deal of the Indian art displayed in museums today is of the deities (gods) and celestial beings of Indian's religions, particularly Buddhism and Hinduism.

As in many ancient cultures, the first Indian art that we know of is rock art on cave walls. Frescoes—large wall paintings also called murals—were discovered in the early 20th century in Indian temples.

Indian folk art and tribal art is still produced in much the same way as it was centuries ago. India exports its pottery, metalwork, paper art, weaving, jewelry, and toys.

One of the most popular forms of Indian art is the age-old custom of Rangoli—sand paintings created with ground white powder and colors. Rangoli is used to decorate floors and walls. People change their Rangoli with the seasons.

Mehndi—henna painting that is a temporary form of tattooing—is an enormously popular body art. Henna is a red-orange dye that comes from the henna plant. Women's and children's hands and feet are decorated with elaborate designs for festivals and celebrations. If left on overnight, the designs can last up to one month.

Indian literature is thought to be some of the world's earliest. Much of it was handed down orally from generation to generation and written down centuries later. Some of India's most famous texts that still provide inspiration today are the Vedas. These are the oldest sacred writings of Hinduism that were written in ancient Sanskrit and are still honored throughout the world.

With so many languages in India, many regions produced famous writers and equally famous literature. But Rabindranath Tagore is the one writer for which all of India is known. He won India's first Nobel Prize for Literature in 1913. However, he was not only a writer! He was a poet, playwright, composer, and visual artist, and is still respected today for his contributions to the art world. He is called the father of modern art in India.

Although Indian kids still read the classics, they're reading popular literature, too. You're likely to find comic books, graphic novels, magazines, and kids' books translated from other languages on their bookshelves.

Music & Dance

Indian music probably began with chanting sacred hymns in Sanskrit. By the 16th century, songs were being composed in Hindi and other languages. Classical instruments included drums, stringed instruments, and wind instruments. By the mid-1700s, violins were commonly used—an instrument Indians still love today. Traditionally, classical Indian music would have been performed in temples and in the homes of the wealthy. Today, people flock to concert halls to hear it.

The British rock group The Beatles brought awareness of Indian music to the world in the 1960s. Ravi Shankar, a famous Indian musician, played the sitar on one of the Beatles' albums. (The sitar is a long-necked Indian stringed instrument with a unique sound.) Shankar has worked with many Western musicians since then and was nominated for an Oscar for co-writing the musical score for the film, *Gandhi*. Indians in the 21st century are likely to be listening to filmi (songs from films), folk music, classical music, rock, jazz, or fusion music that blends the Indian and Western styles.

There are two main types of Indian dance: classical dance and folk dance. Classical dances tell stories with spiritual themes. Centuries ago, classical Indian dancers performed in the temples. Classical dances have been handed down through the centuries. Every one of them has a different meaning. Those who make a career of classical dancing begin training as young as age six! Classical dance festivals are held throughout India every year.

Folk dances originated in the Indian rural areas. Each area of India has its own special folk dances. Many are performed by ordinary people who gather for special occasions, like the yearly harvest or planting. Some of the dances are performed by women, some by kids, and some by anyone who wants to participate.

Indian Celebrations!

Republic Day
January 26

This is India's great national festival, celebrated in the capital of New Delhi and in the states and district capitals throughout the country. The grand parade in New Delhi includes marches of the three Indian Armed Forces and ends with jet planes streaking colored smoke across the sky. Schoolchildren perform various cultural programs. And achievements are recognized throughout the country: children are given Children's Bravery Awards, and soldiers are awarded bravery medals.

Labour Day
May 1

Like Labor Day in the United States, this national holiday in India honors workers. Various labor organizations have processions on this day.

Independence Day
August 15

This national holiday celebrates the day in 1947 when India became free of British rule. The state capitals hold flag-raising ceremonies and cultural programs. The Prime Minister's speech is a highlight of the day. All Indian government organizations are closed. In New Delhi, most of the government offices are lit up. Although students do no schoolwork on this day, students and teachers attend flag-raising ceremonies, sing the National Anthem, and attend cultural celebrations. Families and friends get together for lunch or dinner. You see the colors of the Indian flag everywhere!

Gandhi Jayanti
October 2

All offices and schools close on this national holiday to remember Mahatma Gandhi, who was born October 2, 1869. Called the father of the Indian nation, Gandhi played a special role in helping India achieve independence from Britain. Both the President and the Prime Minister pay special tribute to Gandhi. A prayer meeting is held at Gandhi's memorial in New Delhi and in the various state capitals. Representatives from the religions of India take part in the prayer meetings to honor Gandhi's respect for all faiths. Since Gandhi lived a simple life, the festivities are kept simple and respectful.

Children's Day
November 14

This holiday is celebrated on the birthday of India's first prime minister, Pandit Jawaharial Nehru, who loved children and worked for their welfare all of his life. Children's Day is celebrated all over India, especially at schools. Kids really have a special day! They don't have to wear their school uniforms, and they get sweet treats and watch movies. Schools organize culture programs, and teachers perform songs and dances for the students. Television networks air special children's programs all day.

Christmas
December 25

Even though the majority of India is Hindu or Muslim, Christmas is a national holiday in India and celebrated with as much festivity throughout India as it is in America. Trees are decorated—even though they might be banana or mango trees! Oil-filled lamps glow on rooftops, and churches are decorated with poinsettias and candles.

Name _____   Date _____

Gandhi Timeline

Mohandas K. Gandhi is called the Father of India. His writings on nonviolent protest and his simple way of living have influenced many people, such as the Reverend Dr. Martin Luther King, Jr. and others who have worked for civil rights.

Use Internet sites or other resources to read about the life of this fascinating and much-loved leader. Choose four or five key events from his life, and briefly write them on the timeline below (in the order they occurred).

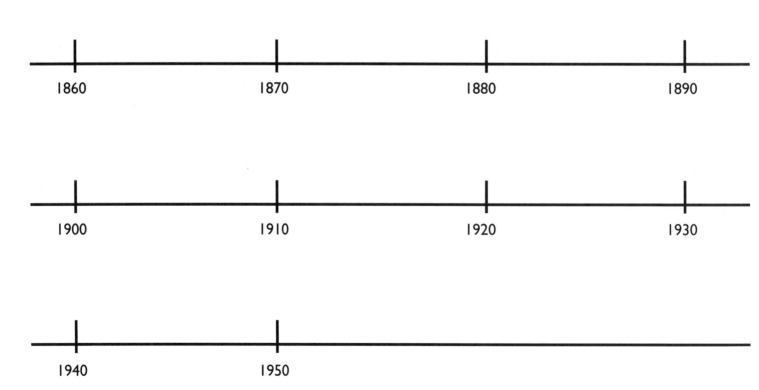

Name _____   Date _____

Indian Food Favorites

Indian food is some of the most delicious in the world, and contains spices, herbs, and ingredients of which you may not have heard. Do some research on the following ingredients and items commonly used in Indian cooking. Write a brief description of each item. If possible, cut out a picture of the food and paste it on the page, or draw the picture yourself. Then choose one of these items, find an Indian recipe that uses it, and write the recipe below the list of food items. Share the recipe with your classmates.

Food	**Description**	**Picture**
cardamom		
chick peas		
cloves		
mango		
okra		
puri		
saffron		
tamarind		

Name _____ Date _____

Try Your Hand at Hindi

About 487 million people in India speak Hindi. It was first spoken in the 4th century B.C.E. and is believed to have evolved from ancient Sanskrit. Try your hand at writing Hindi numbers and their corresponding words.

१	२	३	४	५	६	७	८	९	०
1	2	3	4	5	6	7	8	9	0

Number	Hindi Symbol	Hindi Word	You Try It!
1	१	ek	_____
2	२	do	_____
3	३	teen	_____
4	४	char	_____
5	५	panch	_____
6	६	chhah	_____
7	७	saat	_____
8	८	aath	_____
9	९	nao	_____
0	०	shuny	_____

Write your own math problem using the Hindi symbols above.

Exchange papers with a partner and solve the problem!

FAST FACTS: Japan

Full Name: Japan (Nippon or Nihon-koku)
Capital City: Tokyo
Currency: Japanese yen

Location
Japan can be found in the Pacific Ocean, to the east of the countries of China, Korea, and Russia. Japan is an archipelago, which is a chain or cluster of islands. There are more than 3,000 islands that make up Japan, covering about 146,000 square miles.

The People
Japan is home to approximately 128 million people, giving it the world's tenth largest population. The Yamato people make up a majority of the population, and are considered the native ethnic group of the country.

99 percent of the country speaks the official language of Japanese, a very complex and detailed language. However, English is also spoken throughout Japan. Many of the country's schools teach students both languages.

The Government
The government of Japan is called a constitutional monarchy. The Emperor of Japan has limited power. He is a symbol of the Japanese people, and is trusted with appointing certain government officials, including the Prime Minister. Most power lies with the Prime Minister of Japan. Together with the Japanese parliament, called the Diet, the Prime Minister leads the government. Members of the Diet are elected by the Japanese people, who are given the right to vote when they reach the age of twenty.

The Land
There are four main islands in Japan: Honshu (HAHN-shoo), Hokkaido (hoh-KY-doh), Kyushu (kee-OH-shoo) and Shikoku (shee-KOH-koo). Together, these islands make up 97 percent of Japan's land mass. The country is divided into eight regions and forty-seven prefectures. Each prefecture has a governmental structure, much like our own American cities.

70-80 percent of Japan is covered in forests and mountains. This means that most of Japan is unsuitable for agriculture and habitation. As a result, much of the population is heavily clustered around coastal regions that support farming activities. Japan is also located on the Pacific Ring of Fire, which is known for causing earthquakes and volcanic eruptions. Many of Japan's mountains are actually active volcanoes, including the well-known Mount Fuji.

The Flag
The Japanese flag is a white flag with a large red circle located in the center. The red circle represents the rising sun, a common symbol of Japan, which is sometimes called "the land of the rising sun."

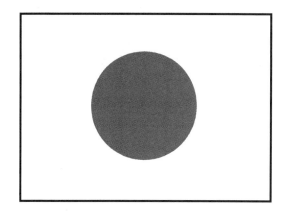

A History of Japan

Early History
Evidence suggests that the region now known as Japan was first occupied around 30,000 B.C.E.. In the thousands of years that followed, many cultures lived in and impacted the region, introducing such concepts as agriculture and writing. The Japanese people were first noted by the Chinese in the Book of Han.

In the eighth century, a time known as the Nara Period, the country of Japan existed with an imperial court located at Heijo-kyo (hay-joh-KEE-oh). This period was followed by the Heian (hay-OHN) Period, which saw the appearance of Japanese art and literature.

The Samurai
The Samurai were a warrior class that ruled Japan beginning in the 12th century. The rulers were called shoguns, and they fought violent battles against invaders and one another to control the country.

In 1603, Tokugawa Ieyasu (toh-kuh-GAH-wah ay-ee-AH-soo) became shogun. Seeking to avoid Western influence, the shogun enacted a policy called *sakoku*, which means "closed country." As a result, Japan developed a distinct culture over the next two hundred years, isolating themselves from the rest of the world. But Japan could not ignore the rest of the world forever.

The Meiji Restoration
In 1854, ships from the United States of America arrived in Japan, ending the era of sakoku. The period that followed is called the Meiji (MAY-jee) Restoration. The shoguns handed over control of Japan to a Japanese emperor in 1867. Japan began to adopt Western ideas, especially industrialization. This angered the remaining samurai, and they attempted to fight the new Japanese empire. They were easily defeated, however, and the samurai all but vanished. Japan quickly became a modern and powerful nation.

Pearl Harbor

On December 7, 1941, Japanese soldiers attacked Pearl Harbor, an American base in Hawaii. This violent surprise forced the United States to enter World War II, and began a fierce and costly period of warfare for Japan. In 1945, the United States dropped atomic bombs on the Japanese cities of Hiroshima and Nagasaki, causing horrible damage and killing countless people. Japan was forced to surrender, and was occupied by American forces for several years.

In the years spanning the 1950s to the 1980s, Japan began rebuilding their nation. They experienced rapid economic growth. They established peaceful relations with the United Stated and the rest of the world.

Modern Japan is an advanced, powerful nation. Their economy is the second largest in the world. But the ancient and unique culture of Japan remains in place. This combination of old and new makes the island nation one of the most interesting countries in the world.

Everyday Japan

Food

The traditional Japanese meal is a combination of rice, soup, and *okazu* (oh-KAH-zoo). Okazu are dishes made from fish, meat, vegetables, or other items that add flavor to the rice. It is the preparation of the okazu that makes a dish special. The dishes are prepared in a variety of ways (raw, grilled, steamed, fried, etc.). Okazu are often made with seafood, as Japan is an island. When the Japanese have had enough rice, they substitute noodles. Noodles are very popular in Japan, especially *ramen*. Ramen are wheat noodles served in broth. But ramen noodles aren't only popular in Japan. You might have seen these noodles at the grocery store!

Clothing

If you were walking around Japan today, their clothing would look a lot like yours. Japanese wear t-shirts, jeans, polos, and many other common modern garments. However, on special occasions, you might catch a glimpse of the ancient national costume of Japan - the kimono.

The *kimono* is a full-length robe, usually made of silk. It falls all the way to the ankles, and has very wide sleeves. It is worn wrapped around the body, and is tied at the back with a wide belt, called an *obi* (OH-bee). They are worn with split-toed socks and traditional footwear, such as *zori* (ZOHR-ee), flat-thonged sandals (much like our flip-flops), or *geta* (GAY-tah), sandals with elevated wooden bases.

Today, kimonos are mostly worn by women, and usually only on special occasions, such as weddings or tea parties, although some elder Japanese still wear them daily.

Sports

Sumo

Sumo is an ancient Japanese sport. It is widely considered the country's national sport. Two wrestlers *(rikishi)* try to force one another outside of a circular ring. While wrestling, the opponents are not allowed to touch the ground with any part of the body other than the soles of their feet. Sumo is a very traditional and highly ritualized sport. Wrestlers even live together in training communities known as *heya* (HAY-ah), and lead strict, disciplined lives.

Baseball

Baseball is by far the most popular sport in Japan. The general rules are nearly identical to American baseball. The highest level of professional baseball in Japan is the NPB, or Nippon Professional Baseball. Some of this league's best players have come to America to play in the major leagues, such as Ichiro Suzuki, Daisuke Matsuzaka, and Kosuke Fukudome.

Martial Arts

While martial arts are considered sports in Japan, with public displays taking place often, they are also considered a way of life for many Japanese, teaching discipline and other important traits. The history of these martial arts can be traced back to the samurai. There is a wide variety of different martial arts, among them *koryu* (KOHR-ee-yoo), *jujitsu,* and *judo,* each with a specific style.

These aren't the only sports practiced in Japan, even if they are the most popular. Recent years have seen a surge in the popularity of soccer, golf, and even automobile racing.

Art and Literature

Japanese art is as old as its language, and found its beginnings in writing. In early Japan, writing was performed with a brush. The practice of painting grew naturally from using the brush often. Painting quickly became the most popular form of artistic expression. Japanese-style painting is known as *nihonga* (nee-HOHN-gah), and is still practiced today.

Another Japanese art form is calligraphy, known as *shodo* or *shuji*. Calligraphy is literally the art of writing, turning the simple act of writing letters and words into a beautiful form of artistic expression. Works of calligraphy can include single words or characters, or whole poems or stories. Creating calligraphy can be a very long process, and the Japanese consider it an art form of its own.

There are many other popular Japanese art forms. Sculpture is often influenced by religion, particularly Buddhism. *Ukiyo-e* are woodblock prints. *Ikebana* (eek-ee-BAHN-ah), the art of flower arrangement, is used in gardens throughout Japan and the world.

Theater is very popular in Japan. There are four main forms of theater. *Noh* (noh) uses masks and costumes to create a very stylish presentation. *Kyogen* (kee-OH-jihn) usually focuses on funny subjects and characters. *Kabuki* (kah-BOO-key) involves singing and dancing, and often presents strange and bizarre stories. *Bunraku* (buhn-RAH-koo) is a form of puppet theater.

Japanese literature dates back to the eighth century, when history books and poetry were created. Books were usually about Japanese life and culture until the Meiji Restoration brought about Western influences. Haruki Murakami is a very popular modern Japanese author. His books have become very popular in America.

A very popular form of literature in modern Japan is *manga* (MAYN-gah), or Japanese comic books. These comic books appeal to all ages and depict a variety of stories. They are often presented in black and white. Manga led to the creation of *anime*, animated television and films that have become wildly popular in Japan and the United States.

Music, Dance, and Games

Music is a big part of modern Japanese society. Much of the music you listen to is also listened to in Japan. Some styles unique to Japan include bubble-gum pop and J-pop, which is band music heavily influenced by Western styles. J-pop is often used in Japanese television and film.

Karaoke is extremely popular in Japan. In fact, it is the most widely practiced activity. In karaoke, an amateur singer sings along to popular music played without lyrics. The singer is given a microphone, and reads the lyrics off of a monitor. The result is very entertaining, and often very funny!

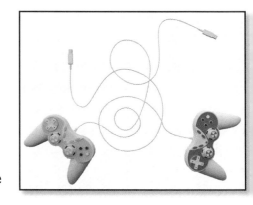

Traditional dances of Japan include *Odori* and *Mai*. Both come from traditional Japanese theater. The *Obon* dance (Bon Odori) is performed during the Obon Festival, a yearly celebration commemorating Japanese ancestors. Another festive dance is the *Sparrow* dance (Suzume Odori), which is based upon the movements of birds. *So-ran Bushi* is a modern dance combining traditional Japanese movements with newer rock music.

Video games are as popular in Japan as they are around the world. Many of the popular games you play are created in Japan. In fact, Nintendo is a Japanese company. They created Super Mario Brothers, among other famous titles.

Japanese Celebrations! (Matsuri!)

New Year (Shogatsu)
January 1st-3rd

The New Year is the most important Japanese celebration. Before the new year arrives, Japanese prepare by cleaning and decorating their homes. They also eat lucky foods, or osechi (oh-SEH-chee), in an attempt to store up good luck for the coming new year. When the day finally arrives, the Japanese celebrate by visiting family, as well as temples and shrines. The festivities last for three days. Lucky games are played to start the new year off right. Examples include karuta (kah-ROO-tah), a card game, hanetsuki (hahn-et-SOO-key), which is a lot like badminton, and the flying of kites.

Coming of Age Day (Seijin no hi)
Second Monday of January

This day is a celebration of all Japanese that have turned twenty during the year. Twenty is an important age in Japan. You are granted to right to vote, and are considered a full adult. Those turning twenty in the particular year are celebrated through special ceremonies.

National Foundation Day (Kenkoku kinen no hi)
February 11

This day is traditionally thought to be the day on which the Japanese nation began. It is now a national holiday that celebrates the Japanese nation and encourages an appreciation and love of the country.

Hanami (Flower Viewing)
Month of April

Japanese celebrate the spring and the beauty of nature in April with flower viewing. Flower festivals take place, as well as picnics and parties dedicated to the viewing of flowers. Flower arrangement is very popular in Japan, and Hanami is one of the biggest events of the spring season.

Golden Week
First week of May

Golden Week is a week of holidays that take place in Japan. Celebrations include:

Greenery Day (Midori no hi)
May 4th

A national holiday celebrating nature, Greenery Day is a day for the Japanese to show their love and appreciation for the gift of nature.

Children's Day (Kodomo no hi)
May 5

This national holiday celebrates children. Families with children decorate their homes, and all Japanese celebrate the spirit and futures of the young.

Bon Festival
August 13th-15th

This festival is an ancient Buddhist tradition. It celebrates Japanese ancestors, whose spirits are supposed to come back to the world on these days. Special altars are set up in homes to welcome ancestor's souls. Grave sites are cleaned and paths cleared to allow the spirits safe passage home. Fires are also lit on the first and last days of the festival, to welcome and send off one's ancestors.

Culture Day (Bunka no hi)
November 3rd

Culture Day celebrates the Japanese constitution, which was announced on November 3, 1946. The day celebrates freedom, and encourages the Japanese to appreciate their culture.

The Emperor's Birthday (Tenno tanjobi)
December 23rd

Based on current Emperor Akihito's birth date, this is a day to celebrate the emperor of Japan. The public is allowed into the Imperial Palace (this only happens twice a year) for a ceremony in which the Emperor and his family appear on a balcony to be congratulated by the crowds.

Name _____   Date _____

Mapping Out History – Japan

Use the map of Japan to record some of the country's historic locations.

1. Tokyo is the capital city of Japan. It is found on the large island of Honshu, directly south of the city of Akita. Locate Tokyo on the map and label it.

2. Label the four main islands of Japan (from northernmost to southernmost island): Hokkaido, Honshu, Shikoku, and Kyushu. Then shade each of the islands a different color.

3. Heijo-kyo was one of the first imperial courts in ancient Japan. It is now known as the city of Nara, and is located north of Hongu. Find Nara on the map, and label it.

4. The eastern coast of Japan borders the Pacific Ocean. Label this body of water and shade it blue.

5. The Sea of Japan is located to the west of the island nation. Label the Sea of Japan and shade it blue.

6. Mount Fuji, an active volcano, is the highest mountain in Japan. It is located along the coast of the Pacific Ocean, on the island of Honshu. Mount Fuji is west of the capital of Japan. Label Mount Fuji on the map.

7. Hiroshima and Nagasaki were two of Japan's largest cities. During World War II, these cities were destroyed by atomic bombs. These events remain one of history's greatest tragedies. Hiroshima is located on the western part of Honshu, and Nagasaki is on Kyushu. Find Hiroshima and Nagasaki on the map, and label these cities.

8. About seventy-five percent of Japan is covered in dense forests and mountains. These regions are found mostly in the interior of the country. Draw mountains and forests throughout the center of Japan.

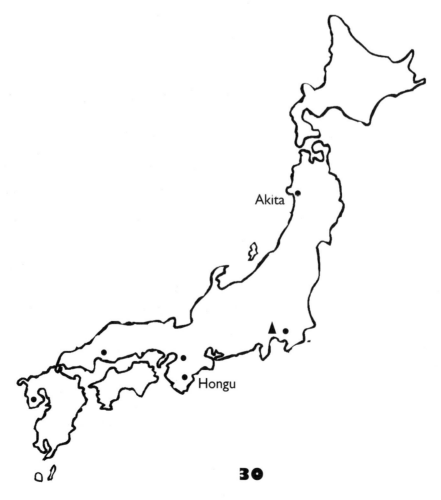

Name _____   Date _____

Haiku

Haiku (hye-KOO) is an ancient and very popular form of Japanese poetry. It is simple in format, made up of three lines and a specific number of syllables (17). The first line contains five syllables, the second line seven, and the third five. You can write a haiku about anything. Read the sample haiku below.

The air is colder
Snow falls slowly from the sky
Winter has arrived

It's easy! Now, try writing a haiku yourself. Remember, the first and last lines can only have five syllables, and the second line can only have seven. Feel free to write your haiku about anything. Have fun with it!

_____

_____

_____

After you finish your first haiku, share it with your classmates. Listen to theirs. Then, try to write some more haiku. Write a haiku about your best friend, or your family. Write one about your favorite school subject. Write one about your least favorite subject. The possibilities are endless!

Title _____

_____

_____

_____

Title _____

_____

_____

_____

Origami

Origami is the ancient art of paper folding. Origami is an art form unique to Japanese culture. The Japanese have been creating origami since the early 1600s. Samurai warriors gave one another works of origami as presents, and weddings were often decorated with different origami pieces.

The goal of origami is to create an object with a single sheet of paper, through a series of folds and creases. Traditionally, no cutting or gluing takes place. Origami designs vary from simple to intricate, from easily created to extremely difficult to make.

One popular origami form is the pelican. Use simple instructions below to make your own origami bird.

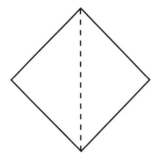

1. Start with a square of paper. Fold in half.

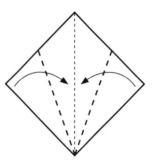

2. Fold in outside corners.

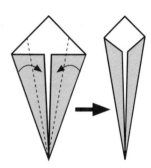

3. Fold in.

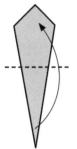

4. Flip over and fold bottom corner up.

5. Fold in half.

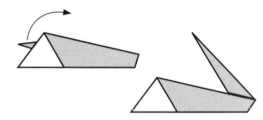

6. Raise the inside triangle. Flatten crease.

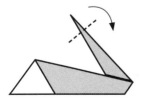

7. Fold the head of the bird in. Flatten crease.

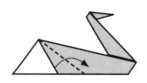

8. Fold each wing up and crease.

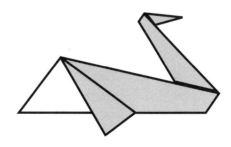

FAST FACTS: Egypt

Full Name: *Arab Republic of Egypt*
Capital City: *Cairo*
Currency: *Egyptian Pound*

Location

Egypt is in northeastern Africa and is an important country of the Arab nation. It is bordered by the Mediterranean Sea to the north, Israel and the Red Sea to the east, Sudan to the south, and Libya to the west. It includes the Sinai Peninsula in northeastern Egypt, the only land link between Africa and the Eastern Hemisphere. It controls the Suez Canal, which allows water transportation between the Indian Ocean and Mediterranean Sea, thus connecting Asia and Europe.

The People

Egyptian civilization began around 3150 B.C.E. The ancient Egyptians achieved many things, including the development of a system for writing and the creation of beautiful art and architecture that endures to this day. Many people living in Egypt today are descended from the ancient Egyptians. The population also includes Africans, Arabs, Greeks, and Turks. Most of the people speak Arabic, which is the official language, according to the Egyptian Constitution.

The Government

Egypt is a democratic Republic with a president who is the head of state. Its Constitution states that Shari'a, the law of Islam (the religious faith of Muslims), is the main source of law. (*Shari'a* (shah-ree-AH) is Arabic for *way* or *path to the water source*.) Egyptian laws are derived from the Qur'an, (koo-RAHN) the holy book of Islam, and from the teachings of the prophet Muhammad. Shari'a covers all aspects of Muslim life in Egypt, from worship to marriage to legal matters.

Egypt's political system includes the executive, legislative, and judicial branches.

The executive branch is composed of the prime minister, his deputies, and the cabinet ministers. The cabinet, which is appointed by the Egyptian president, advises the president on policies that concern the entire nation, such as education, trade, and the environment.

The legislative branch includes the Egyptian Parliament, which is made up of the People's Assembly and the Shura Council. The People's Assembly, the main law-making body in Egypt, is composed of 454 representatives. It is responsible for many things, including writing laws and amendments to the Constitution and overseeing the work of the President. The Shura Council is composed of 264 representatives. The Council is consulted on many things, such as matters regarding Egypt's policies.

The judicial branch includes the Supreme Constitutional Court, along with both religious and secular (nonreligious) courts. This branch of the Egyptian government runs the country's parliamentary and presidential elections.

The Land

Egypt is more than three times the size of New Mexico. The climate is hot and dry in the summer and milder in the winter. As a result of the heat, each spring Egypt suffers from droughts and driving windstorms called khamsin (kahm-SEEN). Dust storms and sandstorms are common.

The Nile River that flows through Egypt is one of its key geographic features and the longest river in the world. Without it, Egypt would have been one vast stretch of desert. People have lived and traveled along the Nile for more than 5,000 years. Of the estimated 75 million people in Egypt, the majority of them still live along the river. The yearly floods from June to September deposit rich soil onto the river banks, which has made this a good farming area for centuries.

The Sahara Desert is the other key geographic feature of Egypt. Also called the Great Desert, it is the world's largest hot desert, covering about 3,500,000 square miles. This includes parts of Northern Africa, from the Red Sea to the Mediterranean coasts, to the outskirts of the Atlantic Ocean.

The Flag

The current Egyptian flag was adopted in 1984. It is composed of red, white, and black horizontal bars. In the middle of the flag is the Eagle of Saladin (Egypt's national emblem that shows a golden eagle facing to the left) above a scroll with the name of Egypt in Arabic.

Red symbolizes a struggle against the British occupation of the country. White symbolizes the 1952 Revolution that ended the monarchy. Black symbolizes the end of the Egyptian people's rule by the monarchy and the British. (See page 35 for more information on the history of Egypt.)

A History of Egypt

Ancient Egypt

The ancient Egyptian culture is thought to be the oldest in the world and is certainly one of the most fascinating and accomplished. It began around 3150 B.C.E. along the Nile River and developed over the next 3,000 years.

The ancient Egyptians were ruled by pharaohs. Most of the pharaohs were men, but a few were women. During their long, rich history, the ancient Egyptians built spectacular pyramids to house the bodies and belongings of their pharaohs. Just how the pyramids were built is still being explored. They developed a system of writing in elaborate symbols called hieroglyphics. They developed a number system. Their doctors were well known healers. Their art is some of the most haunting ever created. On top of all this, they loved to look good, too! Both men and women wore makeup—especially eye makeup that not only outlined the eyes but also protected them from the sun and kept the flies away.

People's fascination with ancient Egypt is stronger than ever. Thousands visit the Sphinx and the pyramids each year. The King Tut exhibit travels the world's great art museums. It features stunning artifacts found in 1922 in the tomb of Tutankhamun, the "boy pharaoh" who became king at age eight or nine and ruled from 1341 B.C.E. to 1323 B.C.E.

The Greek Dynasty

The ancient Greek king and military commander Alexander the Great had conquered most of the known world by the time he died in 323 B.C.E. He made Egypt part of the Greek empire and founded Alexandria as the Egyptian capital.

When Alexander died, his generals set up their own kingdoms. One general, Ptolemy, established the last dynasty that would govern Egypt with a pharaoh for the next 250 years. During this time, Ptolemy made Alexandria the world's center of trade, learning, and culture. The famous Library at Alexandria was built to house millions of scrolls that contained the knowledge of Greek science, art, and literature.

One of Ptolemy's most famous descendants and one of Egypt's best-known pharaohs was Cleopatra VII. This powerful and beautiful queen was intelligent, ruthless, and devoted to Egypt. She died in 30 B.C.E. at the age of 39. People the world over know her name and at least a little of her history. She was the last pharaoh of Egypt. The Greek Dynasty in Egypt ended with her death.

The Roman Era

With Cleopatra's death, Egypt became a province of Rome, which enjoyed all of the benefits of ruling *and* taxing such a wealthy country. Egypt produced crops, glass, paper, and many finer goods that Romans loved, like linen and perfume. Rome ruled Egypt for six centuries. Although few of the Roman emperors ever traveled there or imposed the Roman language and way of life on Egypt, Rome considered Egypt a prize part of the Roman Empire.

The Coptic Era

St. Mark, an African Christian, brought Christianity to Alexandria in the first century B.C.E. and founded the first Coptic Church. (Coptic is an Egyptian language spoken only in Egypt at that time.) Christianity spread across Egypt. It spread so quickly that Diocletian (dy-oh-KLEE-shin), who became Roman emperor in 284 B.C.E., tried to kill many of the Copts. Nevertheless, Coptic Christianity survives to this day in Egypt and in other parts of the world. The Coptic churches are beautiful examples of Coptic art and architecture.

The Islamic Era and Beyond

Muslim Arabs invaded Egypt in AD 639 B.C.E., bringing with them the religion of Islam and the Arabic language found in Egypt today. Muslims ruled Egypt for the next six centuries. They continued to rule even after the conquest of Egypt by the Turks from the Ottoman Empire (what became modern-day Turkey) in 1517.

The French and the English both dominated Egypt at times. Led by Napoleon Bonaparte, the French invaded the land in 1798. After they withdrew, a series of wars took place.

When the Suez Canal was completed in 1869, Egypt became an important world trade center. But the country fell heavily into debt to pay for the canal. Egypt was forced to sell its shares of the canal to Great Britain, which seized control of Egypt in 1882.

Britain quickly eliminated the existing Egyptian government. Constant revolutions by the Egyptian people led Britain to declare Egypt partially independent in 1922. In 1952, Egypt overthrew its British-backed king and became fully independent. In 1953, Egypt became a Republic, and in 1956, Egypt seized control of the Suez Canal. It remains under Egyptian control today. It is open to every nation, and Egypt gets millions of dollars every year from taxing ships that come through the Canal.

Egypt Today

Today Egypt has the largest population in the Arab world. After centuries of invasions and conflict, it still struggles for stability and peace. It has fought with Israel over the Sinai Peninsula. President Anwar Sadat was assassinated in 1981 by terrorists who disagreed with his peace-making efforts toward Israel. But the Egyptian government continues to modernize this vast land. And Egypt continues to draw tourists from all over the world with its beauty and mystery.

Everyday Egypt

Food

The food in Egypt reflects the many cultures of this melting pot land. British, French, Greek, Turkish, and Syrian foods and ingredients are found throughout the country.

Aysh (bread) is served at every meal. The most common aysh is pita bread. A stuffed pita is the Egyptian version of the sandwich.

Egyptians love *ful* (beans)! They boil and then mash them with onions, tomatoes, and spices, and serve them with eggs for breakfast. They cook them into a paste for sandwich fillings. They mix them with spices, form them into patties, and deep fry them.

Ruzz (rice) is a common food item, too. Meat—especially lamb and chicken—is baked into casseroles and served over rice that has been cooked with nuts, onions, and vegetables. Green vegetables and boiled grape leaves are also stuffed with a rice mixture. Fresh fruits like dates and pink oranges are tasty treats among the many fruits available in Egypt year-round. Nuts such as hazelnuts, almonds, and pistachios are common, too.

Egyptian desserts include pastries and puddings drenched in honey, such as *baklava*. Unflavored yogurt is popular, and is sweetened with honey, jam, or mint.

Drinking *ahwa* (coffee) is very common, and coffee bars are found throughout Egypt. Tea is served with milk, lemon, and sugar. *Karkaday,* a native drink served hot or cold, is made from dried hibiscus flowers. Delicious juice shakes are made of fruits such as strawberry, banana, or orange mixed with ice and sugar.

Music & Dance

Egyptian folk music still features modern-day relatives of the percussion instruments, stringed instruments, and cymbals ancient Egyptians played. Egyptian folk dancing, with its brightly colored and exotic costumes, developed primarily in rural villages. Some dances are traditionally performed at ceremonies such as weddings. Others are performed at festivals and tell a joyful story or myth.

Egyptian music in the 21st century is a mixture of influences from Egypt, the Arabian countries, Africa, and Western culture. *Jeel* is one form of Egyptian pop music. Amr Diab is one of Jeel's biggest stars and one of the best-selling Middle Eastern singers of all time.

Sports

We know from drawings in Egyptian tombs that the ancients loved sports and competed in gymnastics, boxing, weightlifting, swimming, rowing, archery, hockey, handball, and marathon running. They had basic rules for their games, and their players wore uniforms.

Sports such as soccer, basketball, handball, and tennis are a vital part of Egyptian culture, and many local sporting clubs receive government money to continue operating. Soccer is Egypt's national sport and creates as much excitement and team loyalty as American football games. Egypt is known for fierce competition in squash (a racquet sport played on a court). It also boasts a total of 24 Olympic medals won since 1928, seven of them gold.

Art & Literature

The unique style we associate with ancient Egyptian art is found on the walls of tombs and elsewhere in Egyptian culture. A person's head was shown in profile (that is, it was seen from the side) instead of facing the viewer. The person's top half faces the viewer, but the feet are shown in profile.

Egyptian pyramids and monuments are some of the world's oldest and largest works of art. The famous Great Sphinx of Giza, a large sculpture with a lion's body and a human head, sits on the west bank of the Nile. This 65-foot-high wonder is thought to be the earliest known monument sculpture. Of course, the famous pyramids, mostly grouped around the city of Cairo, have captivated people for hundreds of years.

Islamic art and architecture abound in Egypt. Because of the strict ban in Islam against showing pictures of humans and animals, Islamic-made rugs, bowls, and vases are decorated with geometric shapes, flowers, and calligraphy. Mosques, places of worship for Muslims, feature slender columns called minarettes that reach into the sky.

Like Egyptian art, Egyptian literature falls into several historic time periods: ancient, Coptic, Islamic, and modern. Although ancient Egyptians had myths, stories, and biographies, much of their literature was meant to help people rather than entertain them. The famous *Book of the Dead*, for example, was written on a papyrus scroll and placed in a person's tomb. It contained hymns, magic spells, and instructions to help the person in the afterlife.

The most famous Coptic literature is the Nag Hammadi Library, 13 early Christian texts found near the town of Nag Hammadi in Egypt in 1945. These leather-bound books were buried in a sealed jar, and it has never been discovered who wrote them or why they were written. The text contains information on early Christianity. The manuscripts are thought to have dated to the third or fourth century B.C.E. They are the oldest known books to date.

After Muslim Arabs conquered Egypt, literature thrived. The Arabs established libraries, replaced papyrus with paper, and introduced calligraphy, which remains a vital part of Egyptian writing today.

Modern Egyptians love novels and poetry. Naguib Mahfouz (1911–2008) won the Nobel Prize for literature in 1988. Many of his works have been made into Arab-language films.

Egyptian Celebrations!

Christmas
January 7

This is a national holiday for Christians and Muslims alike. Coptic Christians celebrate the birth of Christ on this day. Even though Egypt is predominantly Muslim, everyone enjoys the holiday atmosphere. There are Christmas trees in the streets and Christmas lights in people's homes. People gather for a religious service at midnight and have a feast of traditional Christmas festival food called *fata*. Actually, Christmas is so much fun in Egypt that tourists travel from all over the world to enjoy the holiday, Egyptian style!

Islamic New Year
February 10

Compared to the way we celebrate New Year in the West, Islamic New Year is relatively quiet. Muslims gather in mosques for special prayers and readings.

Sham al-Nasseim (shohm ehl-nah-SEEM)
Monday after Coptic Easter

Muslims and Christians alike celebrate this festival to welcome the spring season—one of the oldest local festivals in Egypt. The words *sham al-nasseim* roughly translate to mean *sniffing the breeze*. On this day the ancient Egyptians offered salted fish, lettuce, and onions to their gods. Egyptian families still eat these same foods, along with brightly colored eggs.

Anniversary of the Birth of Muhammad
The Month of May

The celebration of the Prophet Muhammad's birthday in Egypt is like our celebration of Christmas in its excitement and festivities. On this day, Muslims in Egypt deck the streets with lights, hold parades, sing, dance, play music, have children's games and puppet shows, wear new clothes, and get together to eat special foods.

Leylet en Nuktah
June 17

This day marks the rising water levels of the Nile River prior to its flooding each year. In ancient times, a person was sacrificed in the river if the flood was delayed! It was thought that this would appease the river god and bring on the flood so there would be a successful planting and harvest.

Revolution Day
July 23

This is Egypt's national holiday. It celebrates the day in 1952 that three army officers forced Farouk I, the last ruling King of Egypt, to give up his throne. The three officers became the first three Presidents of Egypt.

Ramadan
The Month of August

This is the most blessed time of the Islamic year in Egypt and throughout the world. It is the ninth month of the Islamic year when the Qur'an, the holy book of Islam, was revealed to the Prophet Muhammad. All healthy adult Muslims fast (do not eat or drink) from sunrise to sunset each day during Ramadan. They also reflect on the needs of others and show charity for the needy. At the end of the day, people break their fast with a meal called *iftar*, then visit friends and relatives. Free meals are served outside the main mosques. Many Muslims from all parts of the world visit Egypt during Ramadan.

Eid al-Fitr (eed ehl-FEE-tahr)

This religious festival celebrates the end of the month-long fasting for Ramadan, and it's greatly anticipated throughout the year. Muslims buy new clothes for Eid al-Fitr, exchange gifts, and give sweets to the kids. They attend mosque to pray and to hand out gifts to the needy. They then celebrate with a family lunch when children receive money and new clothes. The entire celebration can last up to five days.

Eid al Adhha (eed ehl-ahd-AH)
70 Days after the End of the Month Ramadan

This four-day religious event, the second of the two Eid festivals in Islam, celebrates Abraham's sacrifice of sheep in the place of his son. People dress in their finest clothing to pray in mosques. There is an effort made to see that no Muslim is left without food during this celebration.

Name _____ Date _____

The Pyramids

The pyramids of Egypt are among the world's oldest and most mysterious structures. Use the Internet and other resources to help you answer the following questions about the pyramids. You may find that not all sources will give you the same answers! Discuss the differences with your classmates, and tell where you found your information.

1. Why were the pyramids constructed? _____
   _____

2. How many known pyramids exist in Egypt? _____
   _____

3. Of what materials were the pyramids made? _____
   _____

4. Where did this material come from? _____
   _____

5. Near what city are most of the pyramids grouped? _____
   _____

6. Who probably built the pyramids? _____
   _____

7. To the ancient Egyptians, what did the shape of the pyramids represent? _____
   _____

8. Why are we so fascinated with pyramids today? _____
   _____
   _____

9. Why do some people think that pyramids were created by aliens? _____
   _____
   _____

10. Would you like to visit the pyramids? Why or why not? _____
    _____
    _____

Name _____ Date _____

A Difference of Customs

In the left-hand column are common customs in Egypt for meeting people, gift giving, and table manners. Read the Egyptian customs on the left, and then write a sentence in the right column to tell how these customs differ from your own. Discuss the differences with your classmates.

Meeting People	
1. Handshakes are customary among members of the same gender.	1.
2. Handshakes are limp and always given with a smile and direct eye contact.	2.
3. Once people know each other well, it is common for men with men and women with women to kiss each other on both cheeks while shaking hands.	3.
Giving Gifts When Invited to Dinner	
4. If you are invited to an Egyptians' home for dinner, bring a gift such as chocolates, but do not bring flowers because these are only given for weddings or to people who are ill.	4.
5. Always give gifts with your right hand or with both hands if the gift is heavy.	5.
6. Your host will not open a gift when he or she receives it.	6.
Table Manners When Invited to Dinner	
7. Wait to be told where to sit at the table.	7.
8. Eat only with your right hand.	8.
9. Take a second helping to compliment the cook and the food.	9.
10. Do not salt your food!	10.

Name _____   Date _____

Translating English to Hieroglyphics

Hieroglyphics were the picture symbols the ancient Egyptians used for their system of writing. Use the provided basic set of Egyptian hieroglyphics to spell the following English words:

1. beetle	
2. cloth	
3. dance	
4. donkey	
5. festival	
6. garden	
7. knee	
8. moon	
9. rest	
10. tent	
Your Name	

*There are many different types of hieroglyphics that have been used throughout history. Different hieroglyphs can represent sounds, words, or even parts of words.

FAST FACTS: Ireland

Full Name: *Republic of Ireland*
Capital City: *Dublin*
Currency: *Euro*

Location
Ireland is an island found in the northwestern part of Europe. To the east of Ireland, across the Irish Sea, is the island of Great Britain. Ireland is the third largest island in Europe, with an area of over 32,500 square miles. It is actually divided into two separate territories. The Republic of Ireland occupies the majority of the land, with Northern Island, a part of Great Britain, located to the north.

The People
Ireland is home to over six million people, most of them (about 4.4 million) in the Republic of Ireland. The remaining 1.7 million Irish live in Northern Ireland, and are subjects of Great Britain.

A native Irish language does exist, though it is rarely used today. It is spoken by a very small minority of Irish people, or at special ceremonies. The official language of the country is English.

The Government
Ireland is governed by a cabinet of seven to fifteen members. This cabinet is given executive authority over the country, and is led by the Prime Minister, called the Taoiseach (TAY-shuhk). The Irish government does have a President. The President is responsible for appointing the Prime Minister and other cabinet members, who are chosen by the Irish parliament.

The Land
Ireland is divided into four provinces: Connacht (cohn-UHT), Leinster (LEHN-ster), Munster, and Ulster. These provinces are further broken up into 32 counties, only six of which lie in Northern Ireland. Remember, Northern Ireland is controlled by Great Britain.

The coasts of Ireland are covered with mountains, while the interior of the island is made up of plains. Ireland is often referred to as "The Emerald Isle." It rains a lot in Ireland, and the climate is very mild. As a result, the entire island is covered with lush, green vegetation.

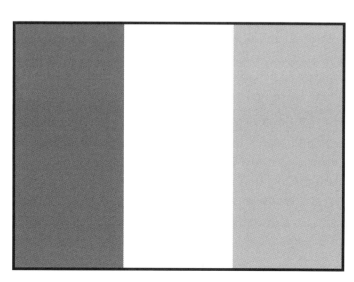

The Flag
The Irish flag is split into thirds, each with a symbolic coloring. The left of the flag is green, and represents the Catholic residents of Ireland. The right side is orange, symbolizing the island's Protestant population. The middle of the flag is white, and is meant to symbolize peace and harmony between the Catholics and Protestants.

A History of Ireland

The history of Ireland is long and violent. The early, peaceful history of the island gave way to a series of invasions and conquests as Ireland was fought over by several countries and cultures. The Irish people were able to withstand centuries of difficulty, however, and established an independent nation.

Early/Pre-Christian Ireland

The first settlement on the island that became Ireland existed around 8,000 B.C.E. Agriculture was introduced to the islanders sometime after 4,000 B.C.E., and the native cultures grew as a result. These cultures were often led by druids, holy men, and teachers. The Irish culture was heavily influenced by a group of people known as Celts (kelts), a culture that existed in ancient Europe and had contact with the Irish island. In particular, the Celts influenced Irish language and development.

Christian Ireland

After centuries of pagan religions and druidic control, the arrival of Christianity in the fifth century swept over Ireland very quickly. Two men are largely responsible for the arrival and spread of the Christian faith in Ireland. Saint Patrick arrived in the early 400s and began converting pagans, while Palladius arrived in 431. Traditionally, Patrick is believed to be the person responsible for the changes that Christianity brought (he was later named the patron saint of Ireland), but history shows that both men were involved.

The arrival and spread of Christianity changed the course of Irish history. It took the place of druidic rule, and ushered in a period of knowledge that helped spread the Irish culture to the rest of the world.

Invasion

In 795, Ireland was invaded by the Vikings from Norway. Towns were destroyed and people were killed. So began a long and violent period for the Irish people. Similar invasions followed, and the Vikings built coastal towns to use as bases for future raids. Some of these towns flourished. Dublin was a Viking town before it was the capital of Ireland.

In 1167, the Norman people arrived in Ireland and began capturing territory. England became involved in 1171, establishing the "Lordship of Ireland." This meant that there were several different groups struggling for control of Ireland. Only one of these groups consisted of native Irish people, but they weren't ready to surrender their country.

Around 1261, forces made up of native Irish began fighting and weakening the Normans. They continued to win back land until 1348, when the Black Death, a horrible plague that killed thousands, arrived and further weakened Norman and English territories. Gradually, and at the cost of many Irish lives, the island came to be dominated by its native residents again.

English Control

In 1563, Henry VII, King of England, decided to take complete control of Ireland and invaded the island. Queen Elizabeth and King James I continued the work Henry started, and eventually England controlled Ireland. The English created a government and forced their Protestant religion on the Irish people. This led to brutal religious wars in the 16th and 17th centuries, as native Irish Catholics rebelled against the Protestant British occupiers. The Irish briefly re-captured control in 1642, but lost it to the English again in 1649. Things were peaceful for some years, but another rebellion broke out in 1798. Again, the Irish were defeated.

After years of war, the Act of Union was established in 1801. This act officially joined Ireland and Great Britain.

The fighting was finally over, but Ireland's problems were not. In 1845, a horrible famine hit the island. Many Irish died, and many more left the island. The famine lasted until 1849, and remains one of the hardest periods in Irish history.

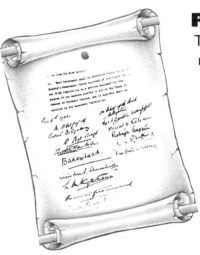

Partition

The Irish were given their own government in 1910. This began a gradual and mostly peaceful surrender of power by Great Britain. An Irish Parliament was elected in 1918, and an Irish Republican Army was created soon after. This led to some violence. In 1921, the Anglo-Irish Treaty was signed, establishing partition, or the division of Ireland into two separate territories. In 1922, Ireland was finally a free state. In 1937, the Constitution of Ireland was signed, and the island was officially named "Ireland." The Republic of Ireland left the British Commonwealth forever in 1949, leaving only the region of Northern Ireland any connection with Great Britain.

Everyday Ireland

Food

Irish food can be broken down into two categories: traditional and modern. Traditional Irish food uses a lot of potatoes. Here are a couple of examples of traditional Irish meals:

Irish Stew - a stew loaded with lamb or mutton, potatoes, onions, and parsley

Irish Breakfast - a fried or grilled dish served with bacon, eggs, sausage, black and white pudding, fried tomatoes and fried potatoes

Modern Irish dishes still use lots of potatoes, but have adopted some different ingredients as well. Seafood has become very popular, particularly shellfish, which are found all along the coast and are of very high quality. Oysters are also eaten, as well as fish, particularly salmon and cod. Bread is a staple in modern Irish cooking.

Sports

Football (Soccer)
Football is very popular in Ireland, and is played at all levels. There are two professional football organizations: Gaelic (GAY-lihk) Football and Association Football.

Hurling
Hurling is an ancient outdoor team sport that has been played in Ireland for centuries. Teams use wooden sticks, called *hurleys*, to hit a small ball, known as a *sliotar* (SHLIH-tehr), up and down a field. Points are scored when the sliotar is hit over or between the goal posts at either end of the field.

Rugby
Rugby was played in Ireland in the 18th century, and is still extremely popular today. Rugby is a team contact sport that has some similarities to American football. A ball is run up and down the field. Defenders attempt to stop the ball carrier. Points are scored by grounding the ball in the opponent's in-goal area, much like a touchdown. You can also score points by kicking goals. Rugby is becoming popular in America, and is played at many colleges.

Other sports played in Ireland include golf, boxing, and horse and dog racing.

Art and Literature

Ireland has been home to some of history's most well known authors. Jonathan Swift, the writer of *Gulliver's Travels*, was Irish. *Ulysses*, written by James Joyce, is one of literature's most famous and studied works. Four Irish writers have been awarded the Nobel Prize, one of literature's most prestigious honors. George Bernard Shaw, William Butler Yeats, Samuel Beckett and Seamus Heaney are all Irishmen that have been honored with the Nobel Prize.

Ireland may be best known for its famous writers, but the island has made a significant contribution to the visual arts as well. Irish art is as old as its civilization, with early inhabitants producing carvings and ornamental gold pieces. Painting became popular in the 19th century, and an impressive collection of work was created by artists such as John Butler Yeats and William Orpen. Ireland is home to many of today's talented artists. Louis le Brocquy and Sean Scully are well-known painters. Ireland offers creative artists special tax breaks, and a large community of aspiring artists live and work in the country.

Music and Dance

Irish folk music is extremely popular, both in Ireland as well as in the rest of the world. It has taken on many forms while maintaining a very distinct sound. Traditional Irish folk music uses various instruments, including fiddles, flutes, pipes, drums and guitars. Music was played at celebrations to inspire dancing, and the two arts became forever linked. More recently, traditional Irish music has been used by artists to enhance their music. Some very popular groups have combined Irish music with rock and roll, for example.

Irish dancing is even more popular than Irish music. It is performed all over the world, and has developed a large audience. Irish *step dance* is performed with traditional Irish music. Dancers keep their upper bodies straight and mostly still, but move their legs very quickly. The result is a very fast and difficult dance that is fascinating to watch!

Irish Celebrations! (Hooleys!)

Saint Patrick's Day
March 17th

Easily Ireland's most important and celebrated holiday, Saint Patrick's Day is a celebration of Saint Patrick, patron saint of Ireland. It is the national holiday of Ireland, but has become extremely popular in the rest of the world. The Irish celebrate by dressing in green clothes. Irish food and drink is consumed, and large celebrations are held all over the country. A five-day festival is held in Dublin, including a giant parade through the city streets.

Easter Monday
Monday after Easter Sunday

Monday is a Christian holiday that is celebrated in many countries, including Ireland. Families and friends gather together to celebrate their faith. Sometimes egg-rolling competitions take place. When celebrating Easter Monday, it might be wise to wear a raincoat. One popular tradition is dousing friends and family with blessed water.

Labour Day
First Monday of May

This holiday celebrates Irish workers and their contributions to the country. It is also sometimes called May Day, a festival that involves singing, dancing, and the decoration of homes with egg shells and flowers.

Samhain (Celtic New Year)
October 31

This festival began thousands of years ago as a day to celebrate the end of the harvest. The Irish lit large fires and prayed to the gods that the sun would return after the winter and allow their crops to grow again. People dressed in costumes to protect themselves from any bad luck. Today, Samhain is more commonly known as Halloween. Irish children dress in costumes and carry lanterns from house to house, asking for treats.

Christmas
December 25th

The Irish celebrate Christmas much like the rest of the world. The insides of homes are decorated with live Christmas trees. After Midnight Mass, children go to bed and wait for Santa to arrive with gifts. Gifts are placed in children's rooms in large sacks. Families and friends gather to celebrate the season.

Saint Stephen's Day
December 26th

A holiday celebrating the life of Saint Stephen, this day is full of tradition in Ireland. It is also known as Wren's Day. Groups of people carry a wren (sometimes a fake one, sometimes an actual live bird) to different houses, singing and dancing, asking for money. Families and friends visit one another as well.

Mapping Out History – Ireland

Use the map of Ireland to record some of the country's historic locations.

1. Ireland is divided into two separate regions, the Republic of Ireland, which makes up a majority of the island, and Northern Ireland, a part of Great Britain. Trace the division between the Republic of Ireland and Northern Ireland with a thick line. Label each region.

2. The capital of Ireland is Dublin, and it is found on the eastern coast. Locate and label the city.

3. Belfast is the capital of Northern Ireland, and it is also found on the eastern coast. Find and label it on the map.

4. Ireland is bordered by the North Atlantic Ocean on its west coast, and the Irish Sea on its east coast. Label these bodies of water and shade them blue.

5. Ireland was plagued with Viking invasions for much of its history. The Vikings established many settlements that have become large Irish cities, including Dublin. Cork, Limerick, and Waterford were all once Viking settlements. Cork is the southernmost city on the map. Waterford is east of Cork, but it is not a coastal city. Limerick is north of Cork and southwest of Dublin. Locate and label these cities on your map.

6. In 1169, the first Norman forces arrived in Ireland. They captured the city of Wexford and went on to control the Irish region of Leinster. Label Wexford, which is east of Waterford.

7. The geography of Ireland is characterized by a ring of coastal mountains, and an interior of lush plains. Label the coastal mountains of Ireland with ∆s and shade them brown. Shade the interior green to symbolize the plains.

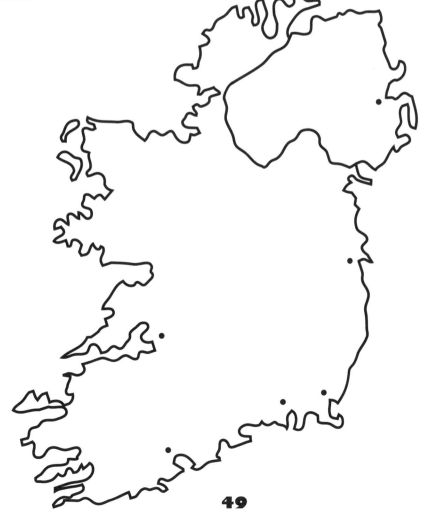

Name _____ Date _____

Limerick

The limerick is a very old form of poetry popularized by the Irish in the 18th century. Limericks were originally written or spoken to describe the adventures of Irish people, and took their name from one such poem, "Will You Come Up to Limerick?" Limerick is a town in Ireland.

There are five lines in a limerick. The first, second, and fifth lines all rhyme, and contain eight syllables. The third and fourth lines rhyme also, and are made up of five syllables each. Read the sample limerick below.

> There once was a young man named Stan,
> Who fancied himself a sports fan,
> He went to the games,
> Knew the players names,
> His job was being Hot Dog Man!

Limericks are often silly poems meant to make readers laugh. It's also very common for the poems to begin with "There once was a...," but they certainly don't have to.

Now it's your turn. Keeping in mind the rules listed above, try writing your own limerick. It can be about anything you want. Try writing one about yourself, or maybe one about your best friend. Share your limericks with your classmates and teachers.

_____

_____

_____

_____

_____

50

Name _____   Date _____

Next Stop: Ireland!

Bring the history and culture of Ireland to your classroom without having to set foot on an airplane! Create an informative travel brochure featuring this historic country to share with your class.

Materials Needed:

- Blank sheet of 8 ½ x 11" paper
- Markers or colored pencils
- Research materials (books, articles, internet access, etc.)

Begin by folding your paper in thirds, as shown:

Use books, magazines, internet articles and other resources to find out more about the many historic cities and landmarks in Ireland. A few examples include:

Bunratty Castle	Belfast	Cliffs of Moher
Dublin	Rock of Cashel	Giant's Causeway
Powerscourt Gardens	Blarney Castle	Killarney

Choose one site or city as the subject of your travel brochure. Illustrate the front cover of the brochure, and write the name of your location. Find the following information about your site and use it to fill the inside pages of your brochure:

1. Where is your landmark located? _____

2. Name three important facts about this site.

   _____
   _____
   _____

3. How is this site important to Ireland's history?

   _____
   _____

4. Why should people visit this site?

   _____
   _____

Include pictures and any other information. Share your brochure with your classmates to learn even more about Ireland!

FAST FACTS: Australia

Full Name: The Commonwealth of Australia
Capital City: Canberra
Currency: The Australian Dollar

Location

Australia is called the "land down under" because it is in the Southern Hemisphere, south of the equator. Like all countries in the Southern Hemisphere, summer is from December to February, and winter is from June to August.

Australia is the world's smallest continent. It comprises the Australian mainland, the island of Tasmania, and many islands in the Indian Pacific Ocean. Indonesia, East Timor, and Papua New Guinea are its neighbors to the north. The Solomon Islands, Vanuatu, and New Caledonia lie to the northeast, New Zealand lies to the southeast. Australia and Tasmania combined are about equal in area to the United States (excluding Alaska and Hawaii).

Australia is an island continent because it is surrounded on all sides by water—primarily the Indian Ocean, the Southern Ocean, and the South Pacific Ocean.

The People

Indigenous (native) Australians include the Aborigines and the Torres Strait Islanders who together make up more than 2.5 percent of the population. Although rich in culture and traditions, the Aboriginal people remained the poorest in terms of jobs and education until the government granted them citizenship and the right to vote in the 1960s. About 350,000 Aboriginal people and 48,000 Torres Strait Islanders live in Australia today. They each maintain their own distinct culture and traditions.

The Government

Australia's form of government is a democracy with a Constitution that protects people's rights and with elected officials who make decisions for the people they represent. It is also a Commonwealth Realm with England's Queen Elizabeth II as its monarch. (You will see Queen Elizabeth's portrait on Australian money, in public buildings, and on postage stamps.)

There are also three branches of government. The legislature, Australia's Commonwealth Parliament, is made up of the Queen, a Senate, and a House of Representatives. The Queen is represented by the Governor-General. The executive branch or Federal Executive Council is made up of the Governor-General who is advised by the Prime Minister and Ministers of State. The judicial branch is made up of the High Court of Australia and other federal courts.

The Land

Of the world's continents, Australia is the flattest and the driest. A large part of it is desert that Aussies (a common term for Australians) commonly call the outback. Mountains run north to south along the east coast. The northern part of the country has a hot, wet tropical climate with rainforests, woodlands, grasslands, outback, and swamps. The southeast and southwest corners have a milder climate. Most of the people on the Australian mainland live along the southeastern coast.

The Flag

The Australian flag was chosen in 1901 as a result of thousands of entries in a worldwide design contest held after the six British colonies of Australia became a federation. The flag has a deep blue background with a Union jack—the flag of Great Britain—in the upper left-hand corner. This shows its ties to Great Britain.

A white seven-pointed Commonwealth Star, called the Star of the Federation, lies below it. Six points of the star represent the original states of the Commonwealth of Australia. The seventh point represents the territories and future states. The right-hand edge of the flag is made up of five white stars—one small five-pointed star and four larger seven-pointed stars. This represents the Southern Cross constellation of stars that is seen in the Southern Hemisphere where Australia lies.

A History of Australia

Australia is made up of many diverse groups who are proud of their heritage. People who are born in Australia are taught tolerance of cultural diversity from an early age. As a result, tolerance and diversity are what draw immigrants to Australia from all over the world, and they continue to shape its history today.

Australia's Indigenous People

The first inhabitants (also called *indigenous* or *native* people) of Australia were the Aborigines and the Torres Strait Islanders. The Aborigines have lived for centuries on the Australian mainland, on the island of Tasmania, and on some neighboring islands. The Torres Strait Islanders came from the Torres Strait Islands between Australia and New Guinea. Researchers think indigenous Australians migrated to Australia 40,000 to 125,000 years ago from Southeast Asia. The Aboriginal culture is thought to be the world's oldest; it is definitely one of the richest in its art and tradition.

From Settlers to Citizens

Australia was isolated for centuries and was only visited by fishermen to the north of the continent. In the 17th century, Dutch, Portuguese, Spanish, and British explorers all made it to Australian shores. In 1770, British Captain James Cook claimed possession of Australia for Great Britain, calling it New South Wales. In 1788, the British set up a colony for prisoners in current-day Sydney. More than 160,000 English prisoners were shipped from England and lived there until the colony was disbanded in 1839.

With more people and more exploration of the land came the establishment of another five colonies in the 19th century: Tasmania, Western Australia, South Australia, Victoria, and Queensland. These, along with New South Wales, were called states and became the Commonwealth of Australia in 1901.

The Australian Constitution combines the traditions of Great Britain and the United States. Some say Australia got the best of both worlds! Australia became known for its liberal laws and its social programs that cared for its citizens, young and old. Although Australia is still a "subject" of Great Britain with loyalty to the British Crown, it has its own laws and policies.

The World Comes to Australia

Australia has always been viewed as a vast land of opportunity. The gold rush and the search for other natural resources drew thousands of people there. The rich land attracted farmers who raised everything from sheep to gain. Before the 1960s, most immigrants to Australia were Irish or English. In the 1960s and '70s, Australia opened its doors to people from other parts of the world, and now about 40 percent of its immigrants are from Asia.

Conflicts all over the world have brought refugees from war-torn countries seeking safety. Some of them have tried to enter Australia illegally. Prime Minister John Howard, who was elected to a third term in 2001, set a tough policy about illegal immigration. About 5,000 people each year—mostly from Afghanistan, Iran, and Iraq—were put in camps and faced a long process to get in the country. Although immigration is an ongoing issue, the government has eased its policies over the years.

Australia Fights!

Particularly during the 20th and early parts of the 21st century, Australians didn't hesitate to fight alongside the United States and Britain. They fought with the British in World War I, and they fought with the British and the Americans in World War II. The Australian military has sent peacekeepers to many other wars, including the 2003 Iraq War.

Australia Today

Australia today is known for mining, food processing, and manufacturing equipment; chemicals, metals, cloth, machinery, and motor vehicles. The country is world-renowned for its diamond and opal mines. Raising livestock, farming, and growing grapes and tropical fruits continue to be important. Australia exports many goods to countries throughout the world, including the United States, China, and Japan.

People from all parts of the world continue to make Australia the multicultural nation it is proud to be. In larger cities, and even in more remote areas, you're likely to see people from many cultures around the world.

Everyday Australia

Food

Everyday Foods

Australians enjoy traditional British foods from recipes handed down by early settlers. People are as likely to tuck into (the British term for "eat with gusto"!) an English steak and kidney pie as they are they are to enjoy the seafood caught off Australian shores. Popular take out (called "take away") foods include fish and chips (French fries), meat pies, sausage rolls (sausage rolled in pastry), and Asian foods. If you get *really* hungry for some American take-out, you can stop for a sub sandwich, a slice of pizza, or a cheeseburger!

Bushfoods

Bushfoods is a general category of foods native to Australia and eaten by Aborigine Peoples centuries ago. These include goanna (Australian lizards) and grubs (the larvae of moths). Bushfood meats still popular today include kangaroo and crocodile. In fact, kangaroo is as popular in Australia as beef is in the United States. As in Britain, lamb is popular, too.

What would your meals be like on a typical day in Australia? For breakfast, you might have bacon and eggs, porridge (a hot cereal like oatmeal), baked beans, grilled tomatoes and mushrooms, fruit, and milk or juice. You might put a dark, salty spread called Vegemite on your toast. Many Australian kids take their lunch to school—and it may look a lot like yours: a sandwich, some fruit, and something sweet. You might stop after school for a special treat like Tim Tams (chocolate cookies). Dinner would be your main meal, and you might have anything from roast beef to a casserole. Your day would probably end with a special dessert like a Frozie Cup (a Popsicle in a cup).

Sports

Australians love sports and outdoor activities, and the country's warm climate makes it easy to participate in both. Cricket (similar to American baseball), rugby, soccer, cycling, rowing, competitive boat racing, swimming, track and field, field hockey, tennis, horse racing, and motor racing—whether people participate in them or watch them on TV—are among the most popular sports. Netball, a game similar to basketball, is the most popular team sport for women. At any international sporting event you will hear the crowd roar "*Aussie! Aussie! Aussie,*" when rooting for their teams.

Australia is no stranger to the Olympics! It hosted the summer Olympics in 2000 in Sydney. Since the late 1800s, Australia has won some 400 Olympic medals, 121 of them gold.

The Australian government gives a great deal of money and support to school sports programs. Australian kids are encouraged to participate in any number of sports—even surfing, water polo, or diving. Chances are, with the wide range of sports programs available, you'd find a sport you loved!

Art & Literature

Much of the art that we think of as traditionally Australian originates with the Aboriginal People. Aboriginal art is some of the world's oldest, dating back 20,000 years or more. Aborigines painted caves, the ground, sacred stones, and even themselves with pictures of people, plants, and animals, and abstract designs like concentric circles. Today Aboriginal People still create beautiful, intricate, and colorful designs of people, places, and animals of the land. Many Aboriginal images are created with hundreds of small dots.

Like Australian artists, Australian writers have been influenced by the vast land and its people. The Aborigines were probably Australia's earliest storytellers, passing down their traditions through storytelling that continues to this day. Banjo Patterson (1864–1941), whose image appears on the Australian $10 bill, was a famous poet, journalist, and writer whose work focused on the outback areas where the indigenous people lived.

The only Australian to receive the Nobel Prize for Literature was Patrick White (1912–1990) in 1973. He used his prize money to establish the Patrick White Award. This is given every year to a creative writer who has written for a long time without a lot of public recognition.

Poetry also has been important to the Australian literary scene over the centuries. Adam Lindsay Gordon (1833–1870) is most famous for his *Bush Ballads and Galloping Rhymes*, published in 1870. He is the only Australian poet to be honored in the famous Poets' Corner of Westminster Abbey in London.

Music & Dance

Australia's modern music scene is much like that of the rest of the world. You will hear just about every type of popular music, including rock, heavy metal, country, jazz, classical, reggae, techno, and hip hop. People love to take their music wherever they go on MP3 players.

You'll still hear the music of the indigenous Australians. The Aborigines continue to create their sacred wind instruments called didgeridoos. These are made from a tree branch hollowed out by termites. Playing one is said to help reduce snoring *and* help you sleep better! Aboriginal rock combines these traditional instruments with the modern guitars and drums.

Dance was important to the rituals and traditions of Australia's indigenous people, and it still plays a major role in Australian culture. Today there are Aborigine and Torres Strait Islander dance companies. There are many ballet and contemporary dance companies, too. Most of the states have youth dance companies. Dance is often a fun part of the hundreds of festivals and celebrations held throughout Australia each year.

Australians in the Movies

Look for some famous Australians in front of the camera! Australian-born movie stars include Nicole Kidman, Russell Crowe, and Cate Blanchett. You may know Paul Hogan better by his film name: Crocodile Dundee. And although he was born in America, Mel Gibson moved to Australia at age 12 and spent much of his early life and film career there.

Australian Celebrations!

No matter where they live, one thing is sure: Australians love to celebrate! While most states and territories observe the same public holidays, others have special celebrations just for their own areas. Here are major celebrations common to all Australians.

Australia Day
January 26th

This holiday celebrates the founding of the first settlement in Australia. The sunny summer January weather makes it easy for Australians to gather throughout the country for concerts, barbeques, ceremonies, or a day at the beach.

Harmony Day
March 21st

This day celebrates harmony and cultural diversity. Local communities put on special events that highlight understanding and respect. In past years, some Harmony Day student activities have included releasing balloons with messages of hope, creating a school jigsaw puzzle with each student contributing a piece, and designing postcards with a harmony theme.

Easter
March or April

Easter in Australia is a four-day holiday, beginning with Good Friday and ending on Easter Monday. Festivals, football matches, boat races, horse races, weddings, and athletic events are held during this period of time. The Easter bunny delivers chocolates and other sweets to Australian children early Easter morning, just as he does to children in other parts of the world. Easter egg hunts are common, too.

ANZAC Day
April 25th

ANZAC Day is similar in purpose to America's Memorial Day. On April 25, 1915, the Australian and New Zealand Army Corps (ANZAC) landed at Gallipoli in Turkey during World War 1. Today this holiday honors the memory of those who fought for Australia and those who lost their lives during any war. Customs include ceremonies at war memorials and military parades.

Melbourne Cup Day
First Tuesday of November

This is Australia's most popular Tuesday of the year. Everyone tunes their TVs to the Melbourne Cup, a world-famous horse race. People in Melbourne get the day off to celebrate. Those lucky enough to attend the actual race make a day of it—and a fashion show of it—by wearing their best clothes and, for the ladies, big hats!

NAIDOC Week
Begins the Second Sunday in July

This week celebrates the heritage of the Aboriginal people and the Torres Strait Islanders. People celebrate in their own communities by inviting people to speak at schools, listening to indigenous music, and studying aboriginal arts and crafts. NAIDOC stands for 'National Aborigines and Islanders Day Observance Committee'.

Australian Citizenship Day
September 17th

Australians celebrate the importance of Australian citizenship on this holiday that began in 2001. Special events include citizenship ceremonies, picnics, barbeques, lunches, and dinners. Those eligible permanent residents who live in Australia but are not yet citizens are encouraged to become citizens so they can enjoy all the benefits of living in the country.

Christmas
December 25th

Christmas is one of the main public holidays in Australia. While we commonly think of it as a cold, snowy day, in Australia it occurs during the early summer heat. Many Australians spend Christmas at the beach or at a campground. Cold turkey, ham, seafood, and salads are served, along with special desserts, such as ice cream pudding. Gifts, greeting cards, carols, and Christmas trees round out the celebration.

Name _____   Date _____

Create Your Own Flag

On page 53 you learned that the Australian flag contains these significant images:

- The Union Jack to symbolize its ties to the British Commonwealth
- The Commonwealth Star to symbolize the original states of the Commonwealth of Australia as well as the territories and future states
- A constellation of stars that can be seen in Australia

Think about two or three things that symbolize your background, your life, your future, or your environment. Draw them in the rectangle below to create your own personal flag. You might consider creating a symbol for any of the following:

- Your family
- Your culture
- Your neighborhood ties
- The state or city in which you live
- Something you love to do
- Something you hope to accomplish

Now add color to your flag. What do your colors symbolize?

Name _____ Date _____

Australian Phrases

In talking to an Australian, you will probably hear some words and phrases not used in other countries. Since early Australian settlers were from Great Britain, many uniquely English phrases crept into the Australian vocabulary. See if you can match the popular terms in the left-hand column to their meaning in Australian English on the right.

1. _____ ketchup
2. _____ McDonald's restaurant
3. _____ cookie
4. _____ broken
5. _____ French fries
6. _____ cantaloupe
7. _____ lemonade
8. _____ root beer
9. _____ footy
10. _____ utility vehicle
11. _____ good friend
12. _____ barbeque
13. _____ a present or gift
14. _____ mosquito
15. _____ chocolate

a. biscuit
b. lemon squash
c. ute
d. barbie
e. mozzy
f. chokkie
g. bunged up
h. football
i. tomato sauce
j. sasprilla
k. mate
l. prezzy
m. rock melon
n. chips
o. Maccas

60

Name _____   Date _____

Creating Symbols

The art of the Aborigines is some of the most unique art in the world. Here are some common symbols used in traditional Aboriginal art that represent words in that language.

Rain   Footprints

Campsite   Digging Stick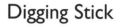

Man U   Emu (a large Australian bird) ↓

Boomerang ⌣   Star ☼

Rainbow or Cloud

Create a list of at least five common things in your classroom, in your home, or in your community, such as book, door, or even the cafeteria! Write the words below and create a simple symbol for each. Share your symbols with the class.

61

Extension Ideas and Additional Resources

Mexico

- Read and discuss a traditional Mexican folktale with your students. Ask the students, *what is a folktale? Why do you think this folktale was written?* Discuss the specific characters and their actions in the story. These books contain a variety of Mexican folktales:
    - Horse Hooves and Chicken Feet: Mexican Folktales, selected by Neil Philip, Clarion Books, 2003.
    - The Day It Snowed Tortillas, by Joe Hayes, Cinco Puntos Press, 2004.

  After you have finished with the story, encourage your students to write their own folktale.

- Plan a fiesta with your students based on a Mexican holiday. Decorate the classroom in red, white, and green for Mexico's Independence Day, make skeletons to hang for Día de los Muertos, or break open a *piñata* at a *posada*. Check out these websites for additional ideas:
    - http://www.mexonline.com/holiday.htm
    - http://www.fundraiseralley.com/teachers/fiestatips.html
    - http://www.crayola.com/calendar/ (Events are listed throughout the year)

- In the spirit of Diego Rivera, David Siqueiros, and Jose Orozco, have the students create a mural depicting the history of your class. Using a large sheet of brown craft paper and markers, have each student draw a picture of their favorite event since the beginning of the year. It could be of a field trip, a particular lesson, a special school event, or even a favorite book that was read. Hang the mural in the classroom or hallway for all to enjoy.

India

- Many people in India, no matter where they live or work, wear traditional Indian clothing at least some of the time. Bring in pictures of traditional Indian clothing (or bring in actual items of the clothing, if possible), including:

  For women:
    - the sari
    - the salwar-kameez and dupatta
    - the lehenga, choli, and odhani

  For men:
    - the dhoti
    - the kurta
    - the sherwani

  Have students compare the clothing of their own traditional cultures with the Indian clothing. What similarities and differences do they notice? How does physical environment influence what people wear?

- One of the most popular art forms in India is Rangoli. These colorful designs are painted on the ground in front of people's homes as a friendly sign of welcome. Rangoli designs are simple or intricate and revolve around theme such as plants or animals. These sites offer templates and further information on Rangoli designs.
    - http://www.dltk-kids.com/World/india/mrangoli.htm
    - http://freerangolidesigns.blogspot.com/

  Reproduce a few Rangoli design templates for your students to color using crayons, oil pastels, colored pencils, or paints. Decorate the entrance of the door of your classroom with students' images.

- Indian customs are some of the best observed, yet probably some of the least understood in the world. Discuss with students the meaning of the following Indian customs:
    - Namaste (the popular form of greeting used to welcome or to say goodbye)
    - Tilak (the ritual mark on the forehead)
    - Arati (rotating a lamp-lit tray in front of a person or a deity in an act of welcome)
    - Flower garlands (offered to visitors)
    - Bindi (a red dot worn by girls and women on the forehead)
    - Nose pin (worn generally by married women)

  Have students research more about these customs and compare them with customs from their own cultures.

Japan

- One of Japan's most popular forms of entertainment is theater. Japan is known for four distinct, unique kinds of theater.
    - Noh: stylish use of masks and costumes
    - Kyogen: funny characters and plots
    - Kabuki: strange stories presented through singing and dancing
    - Bunraku: puppet theater

  Divide your class into four groups. Assign each group a different kind of Japanese theater. Using the internet or other available resources, have the group members research their particular genre. Task your students with creating a short play using the traditions of their particular group. Provide help as they write their plays and plan their presentations. Let the students act out their plays for the rest of the class.

- Japan is a breathtakingly beautiful country bursting with sights, and a popular tourist destination. Have your students plan an imaginary vacation to Japan. Let students research the many attractions and design their own itinerary. Where do they want to visit? What do they want to see? Why? Have students present their travel plans to each other, and discuss their choices and the reasons behind them. Here are some websites to start your students on their research:
    - www.jnto.go.jp/eng
    - www.web-japan.org/kidsweb
    - www.japan-guide.com/e/e623html

- The origami activity on page 32 doesn't even scratch the surface of the art form! There are more designs and variations than you can possibly imagine. Continue your class's exploration of this ancient Japanese art form. Bring in several origami designs and their instructions and let your class choose which ones to attempt. You will need to provide materials (paper). Encourage your students to research origami on their own, as well. Let them bring in their completed projects to share. Here are some sites where you and your students can find origami information and instructions:
  - www.origami-club.com/en
  - www.origami-fun.com

Egypt

- The Rosetta Stone is a famous Ancient Egyptian artifact that has been on display almost continuously at the British Museum since the early 1800s. Have students research and discuss what the Rosetta Stone is, how it was found, who found it, what it says, and how the writing on the stone helped people understanding the meaning of hieroglyphics.
- The Bedouin Arab tribes in the Eastern Egyptian deserts and the Sinai Peninsula are a nomadic people of the Middle East with ancient roots. Have students research and write a few paragraphs on the nomadic life of the Bedouin tribes, including where they are primarily located in Egypt, how they survive in the desert, their family life, and their tribal structure. These websites offer interesting insights:
  - http://www.touregypt.net/featurestories/bedouins.htm
  - http://www.geographia.com/egypt/sinai/bedouin02.htm
- The ancient Egyptians believed in placing statues, jewelry, clothing, utensils, pictures, and other objects of everyday life in a deceased person's tomb to help him or her live well in the afterlife. Have students look for pictures of the many objects found in Egyptian tombs and draw some of these objects. Have them label their images and display them around the classroom.

Ireland

- Irish dance is an enormously important part of Irish history and culture. The Irish have been dancing for centuries, and their steps and music have become a worldwide phenomenon. To introduce this form to your class, look into the history behind Irish dance with your students. Use the internet (www.irelandseye.com/dance.html) and other resources to gather some general history. Next, try some simple steps. Keep in mind that Irish dance can be rather complex; patience is a must! Here are some websites that provide basic instructions.
  - www.irelandseye.com/aarticles/culture/music/dance/steps.shtm
  - www.learntodance.com/online%20irish%20dancing%20lessons.htm

Try the dances without music. Let students get a feel for the steps. After a few practice runs, try playing some traditional Irish music. Don't put too much emphasis on form. Let the students dance their own Irish jigs!

- A coat of arms is a symbol that tells about the person or family it represents. It usually consists of a shield emblazoned with symbols. Ireland's coat of arms is a gold harp with silver strings on a blue background often referred to as Saint Patrick's Blue. The harp is a very old symbol of Ireland. Have students design their own coat of arms. Encourage them to think of things that they really enjoy and what pictures could be used to symbolize them. Provide materials (construction paper, markers, etc.) and urge students to be creative. Let each student share his or her finished coat of arms with the rest of the class, explaining his or her symbols and colors.
- Have you ever heard of "the luck of the Irish?" Ireland has a lot of myths and superstitions involving luck. There are several popular Irish symbols and stories concerning luck:
  - Leprechauns: These small fairies hide from humans and protect buried treasure. But if you're lucky enough to find one, you can supposedly follow him to his treasure, found at the end of a rainbow.
  - Four-Leaf Clovers: You may never see a leprechaun, but it's very possible (though uncommon) that you'll see a four-leaf clover in your life. These rare green plants are supposed to bring good luck when discovered.
  - The Blarney Stone: Set in the stones of a castle in Ireland, those who kiss this rock are gifted with eloquence and good luck for the rest of their lives. Tourists from all over the world flock to kiss this stone!

Have your students research these and other lucky charms from Ireland. Compare them with modern symbols of good luck.

Australia

- The Sydney Harbour Bridge is a famous Australian landmark and the world's largest steel arch bridge. Climbing to the top of this monument has become a tradition for visitors from around the globe. Have students research the Sydney Harbour Bridge climb and how tourists get to the top of the bridge safely. Here are some websites that offer information on this world-famous attraction:
  - http://www.bridgeclimb.com
  - http://www.pylonlookout.com.au/
  - http://www.sydney.visitorsbureau.com.au/page2-03g.html
- The Great Barrier Reef lies in the Coral Sea off the coast of Queensland in northeast Australia. Built by tiny coral polyps, the reef is the world's largest single structure made by living organisms. Have students work in small groups to research the Great Barrier Reef and create a one-page tourist brochure that includes the following:
  - Some background on how the Reef came into existence
  - The diversity of life it supports
  - Its beauty as a tourist attraction
  - Types of excursions a tourist could take to the area (for example, a glass-bottomed boat tour or a scuba diving expedition)

◯ Divide the class into small groups. Have the students in each group choose a total of five or more of the symbols they developed for the Creating Symbols Activity on page 61. Then have each group work together to put its symbols in order to create a story about anything that develops from the images.

- For example, if a student group used symbols for *boy, girl, book, cafeteria, cookie,* and *money,* a story could evolve about students eating together in the cafeteria when one student suddenly gets a craving for a cookie and finds he has no money to buy one.
- Allow the stories to be fun, frivolous, or serious—whatever evolves from the use of the symbols. Students can write their symbols on the board or on a piece of paper. Then have each group present its story, showing the symbols in order during the storytelling, to the rest of the class.

◯ Kangaroos, koala bears, lorikeets, the platypus, the echidna, the emu, bandicoots, wallabies, wombats, and the kookaburra are just some of the exotic creatures found in Australia. Have students research at least one of the fascinating creatures found exclusively in Australia and describe it, its habitat, and anything that makes it interesting, unusual, or exciting to observe. Here are some good resources on Australian animals:

- 30 Amazing Australian Animals by Christopher Cheng, Random House Australia, 2007
- Tracks, Scats and Other Traces: A Field Guide to Australian Mammals by Barbara Triggs, Oxford University Press, 1996
- Look What Came from Australia by Kevin Davis, Franklin Watts, 2000

Answer Keys

Mathematics... Mayan-Style! Page 11

Addition   Subtraction   Multiplication   Division

Mapping Out History - Mexico Page 12

Indian Food Favorites Page 22

cardamom: a spice that is a member of the ginger family
chick peas: large round peas also called garbanzo beans
cloves: a dried flower bud sometimes used whole or ground into foods, and sometimes eaten after a meal to freshen the breath
mango: a large, tropical fruit with a smooth skin, juicy pulp, and a big seed
okra: a long green vegetable full of seeds—it's also called ladies fingers
puri: a deep-fried flat bread that puffs up when cooked
saffron: a golden-yellow spice that comes from the stamens of the crocus flower
tamarind: a sweet and sour fruit that develops in pods

Mapping Out History - Japan Page 30

What Do I Know About the Pyramids? Page 40

1. as tombs for Egyptian pharaohs
2. about 110—some of them are almost unrecognizable
3. granite and limestone
4. quarries
5. Cairo
6. Egyptians who lived in local villages that were built and governed by the pharaohs
7. the rays of the sun or the mound of dirt from which the Earth was created
8. Answers will vary.
9. It seems impossible that this overwhelming amount of work could have been done in a time when there were so few mechanical advances to lift the stone into place.

Answers will vary.

Mapping Out History - Ireland Page 49

Australian English Page 56

1. i	6. m	11. k
2. o	7. b	12. d
3. a	8. j	13. l
4. g	9. h	14. e
5. n	10. c	15. f